WAR FOR THE WORLD

VOLUME 54
THE CHRONICLES
OF AMERICA SERIES
ALLAN NEVINS
EDITOR

AIR DEFENSE: BATTLE OF SANTA CRUZ

From the water color by Dwight C. Shepler, Commander U.S.N.R.

WAR FOR THE WORLD

A CHRONICLE OF
OUR FIGHTING FORCES
IN WORLD WAR II
BY FLETCHER PRATT

NEW HAVEN: YALE UNIVERSITY PRESS
TORONTO: GLASGOW, BROOK & CO.
LONDON: GEOFFREY CUMBERLEGE
OXFORD UNIVERSITY PRESS
1950

CONTENTS

CONTENTS

ILLUSTRATIONS

ILLUSTRATIONS

WAR FOR THE WORLD

∴

CHAPTER I

THE JAPANESE ATTACK

AT 7:55 on the morning of December 7, 1941, the full air groups from six Japanese carriers appeared simultaneously over Pearl Harbor and the various air bases on Oahu Island in the Hawaiian Islands. At 7:58 the bombs began to drop and the commander of the naval air station shouted into a radio transmitter powerful enough to carry far across the Pacific: "Air raid on Pearl Harbor! This is no drill!"

At that moment, while two Japanese "peace envoys" were handing to Secretary of State Cordell Hull a note which caused that usually reserved old gentleman to turn white with rage, the United States had eight of its fifteen first-line battleships at anchor in the harbor, just preparing for the morning raising of the colors and the ceremonies incident upon beginning a day of rest. Seven cruisers were with them, and three destroyers were in dry dock. Many of the crews were ashore, the officers at the Royal Hawaiian presumably sleeping off the effects of the previous night's festivities, the enlisted men in somewhat less pretentious establishments.

Of the remaining battleships one was near Puget Sound, while the other six were in the Atlantic, where German submarines had been making an active but undeclared war on us and had already torpedoed three United States warships. Four of the seven aircraft carriers were also in the Atlantic; so were several of the 37 cruisers and a large number of destroyers. Two of the other carriers were far to the west of Hawaii under cruiser escort, one of them having just delivered some Marine planes to the outpost at Wake Island; one carrier was at San Diego.

In the Philippines we had one heavy cruiser, an old and a new light cruiser, 12 old destroyers and 29 submarines, beside 30 patrol planes. All had been alerted for some time and were in a good state of readiness for war but short of crews. The supporting industrial machine had been set in motion by the war in Europe and a fleet outnumbering all the ships afloat was on the ways, but beyond two new battleships already running their shakedown cruises, nothing larger than a destroyer would join the battle line for a year to come.

The army was mostly scattered through training

camps in the Southern states. Following the Draft Act of 1940, it had been rapidly expanded from its pre-war strength of approximately 200,000 men to some 72 divisions, but the process involved the distribution of experienced soldiers throughout the mass, and fusion was still far from complete, as autumn maneuvers in Louisiana and the Carolinas had demonstrated. The production machinery of the nation had been thrown into high gear, but the military articles produced had mainly gone to Britain, and there were grave shortages in tanks, heavy artillery, planes, and even rifles. American troops were in Iceland and construction work was in progress on a chain of sea and air bases from that point along the Atlantic to Trinidad, title to land having been acquired by lease from England in exchange for fifty old destroyers. None of these bases was as yet complete.

THE Japanese attack on Pearl Harbor was planned with great care and was extraordinarily successful, being much aided by two factors. One was the neat American method of lining up planes wing to wing across an airfield. The earliest waves of attack fell on these parked planes and the runways from which they might have operated. When Rear-Admiral Bellinger of the Naval Air Force tried to get planes off at the height of the attack, he found only three out of 202 capable of flight.

The army record was approximately the same, nearly all of its 273 planes being wrecked in this first rush.

The second factor was careful Japanese scouting, partly no doubt by spies, but more immediately by midget submarines with two-man crews, one of which was sunk at the entrance to the harbor by the destroyer *Ward* just before the attack came in. At least two other midgets got into the harbor and made a complete tour of it. The information they transmitted was not altogether accurate but it was sufficient for the Japanese dive bombers and torpedo planes that followed the first wave to come in without hesitation on the battleships as they lay moored in a long double row beside Ford Island at the center of the harbor. The enemy planes were armed with heavy armor-piercing shells to which wings had been affixed for bombing purposes and with a specially designed torpedo of very short run and high explosive power.

The battleship *Arizona* got one of the bombs either through a turret or down her stack. It reached the forward magazines and she blew up. The battleship *Oklahoma* capsized as the result of several torpedo hits; *West Virginia* received no fewer than six torpedoes and settled to the bottom with her decks awash; *California* similarly settled, her fuel tanks ruptured and the ship ringed with fire; *Pennsylvania* had a bad bomb hit forward and was further damaged when two destroyers in the dock with her went up in flames and exploded; *Maryland* had two heavy bomb hits and settled by the head. Of the remaining battleships, *Tennessee,* not much damaged, was wedged against a dock by the sunken *West Virginia. Nevada* got underway to stand out at the harbor, but this made her a target for every Japanese plane in the vicinity and she was so badly hit that she had to be beached in the entrance. Three of the light cruisers were seriously damaged, another destroyer had her bows blown off, and the mine layer *Oglala* was sunk. So was the target-ship *Utah,* which had erroneously been reported as a carrier by the Japanese scouts and so received one of the heaviest attacks of all.

The immediate price of their treacherous victory to the Japanese was fifty-odd planes shot down during the action, about half by army pursuit ships that succeeded in taking the air. On the American side, the American Pacific Fleet had practically ceased to exist, and a new command setup had to be made on the spur of the moment, since neither the public nor their own officers would have any confidence in the leaders who had been so taken by surprise—Admiral Husband E. Kimmel of the Pacific Fleet and Lieutenant-General Walter Short of the Hawaiian Command. It was obvious that the Philippines could not be held. There was nothing in existence that could interfere with a Japanese

intention to put in as many as fifty divisions, if
necessary, against the two-division strength that
held the islands. The Pacific question, in a military sense, was purely one of whether the Japanese
could be restrained from the conquest of Australia.
Meanwhile the President was preparing a declaration of war which was voted on the morning of
December 8, over the odd objection of a single
member that the news from Pearl Harbor might
not be true. It was also obvious that the Germans
and Italians would come into the war against us,
and that we should have their submarines in numbers off the Atlantic coast; possibly their airplanes
over our cities.

There was a conference at the White House on
the afternoon of the 7th and another at the Navy
Department immediately. President Roosevelt
brought in Admiral Ernest J. King from the Atlantic Fleet in the dual capacity of commander
of forces afloat and Chief of Naval Operations. To
Honolulu he sent Admiral Chester W. Nimitz, head
of the Bureau of Navigation (Personnel), who was
something of a specialist in personnel relations and
could be counted upon to pull up the badly shat-
tered morale of the fleet.

The carriers at sea were ordered toward the Japanese-held Marshalls, in which direction it was supposed that the enemy had gone. *Yorktown* and
Hornet, carriers, were ordered from the Atlantic

and *Saratoga* from San Diego to make near Pearl Harbor a concentration that would have to bear the weight of the war till the battleships could be repaired. A number of big bombers originally destined for England were dispatched to Honolulu and so were all the navy patrol planes from the Pacific coast. An emergency appeal for shipyard workers to repair the damaged vessels was sent out (they had three of them at sea before Christmas); the army stepped up both its draft and its industrial programs; and by December 11, when Hitler's Germany followed Japan into war with the United States, there were already troopships on the tide bound westward.

RADIO TOKYO, which was later to develop so high an index of inaccuracy, announced on the morning after the attack of December 7, 1941, that five of our battleships had been destroyed and three of the carriers damaged beyond repair. From subsequent events it is evident this did not represent propaganda so much as a genuine Japanese appraisal of the result they had secured. They captured Guam on the third day of the war from a garrison less than 600 strong. Wake Island with the aid of the Marine planes held out until December 22 and acquired a considerable symbolic importance, but after it fell there was no longer any American post within the width of the Atlantic from Japan, and the enemy felt secure against any counterattack for a long time to come.

His primary objective was the capture and exploitation of the supply storehouse of the East Indies, and he now turned in that direction without fear of interruption, since his attacks on American installations had succeeded in so immobilizing our forces that no counterattack was possible. French Indo-China had been seized earlier in the year, and a large portion of the Japanese fleet was based there. Simultaneously with the attack on Pearl Harbor Japanese planes struck at the British base at Singapore, though in smaller numbers and doing less damage, and a Japanese landing force was thrown on the northern shore of Malaya at Khota Baru. At the same time there were Japanese scout planes all around and over Luzon, and Davao in the southern Philippines was heavily attacked. But something went wrong with the timing, and the enemy made no effort against the stronger installations around Manila until nine hours after word of Pearl Harbor had reached both Admiral Thomas C. Hart of the Asiatic Fleet and General Douglas MacArthur of the Army in the Philippines.

The warning did not do much good. When the planes came in at noon on December 8 (10 hours after the attack on Pearl Harbor, but a day later by International time) they found that the army planes had flown one futile search mission and had lined themselves up on Clark and Nichols Field. Later, it was protested that dispersal areas were lacking, but the responsibility both for this and for the neat alignment rests rather clearly on General Douglas MacArthur as Area Commander. Secretary of War Stimson had written in a report not published till the turn of the year that the army intended to place "radical reliance" on the air arm for the defense of the islands. The pilots were our best, the planes new, and very good. Two thirds of the fighters and more than half of the bombers were destroyed in that first smash; and after the Japanese forced a landing and got an air strip established at Aparri at the northern tip of the island, they rapidly wore the rest of our aviation out by mere continuous action.

To complete the disasters of the day, a heavy force of Japanese bombers and torpedo planes caught the British battleships *Repulse* and *Prince of Wales* off the coast of Malaya without air cover and sent them to the bottom, the only heavy ships the Allies had in the East. The next day Japanese bombers either from Indo-China or carriers out at sea swept in deliberate procession across the navy yard at Cavite. There were no fighters to disturb them, and keeping above the fire of the old-model short-range anti-aircraft guns, they patiently reduced the place to rubble, sinking an American submarine during the process. In the initial moves of the campaign the Japanese had driven our air force from the skies and our navy from the seas around the Philippines, at almost no cost to themselves. Now they came storming ashore at Vigan on the northwest coast of Luzon and along the southern peninsula of Legaspi to close in on Manila and trap MacArthur there.

The Lingayen Gulf landing (Vigan) was the heaviest, about 80,000 strong; this alone was far more than MacArthur's whole force. The invaders had so complete a control of the air that counter-attacks had to be local and delivered only by night, but the American lines held fairly firm till December 24, when still another Japanese force was put ashore on Batangas Peninsula, south and west of the capital. A Japanese break-through on any of the thinly held fronts would now expose the forces on all the others to being taken in the rear. MacArthur declared Manila an open city. In accordance with a plan drawn several years before by a young staff officer called Major Dwight Eisenhower, MacArthur held hard in the fertile valley that runs from Lingayen to Manila, while drawing his forces from the other fronts to form a concentration on Bataan Peninsula.

The operation was beautifully executed and was complete by January 1, but meanwhile the Japanese savagely bombed Manila on several occasions, showing a preference for Sundays when they would

catch the maximum number of people in churches
and arouse the greatest terror. They continued to
put men ashore on Luzon till there were not far
short of 250,000, but their difficulty was in using
this large force effectively. Bataan is occupied by
the Mariveles Mountains, which run so steeply to
the sea along their western slope that it is often
necessary to wade into the water to progress from
north to south, while on the eastern, valleyward
flank there is only a narrow cultivated zone between the mountains and the extensive swamps
which covered MacArthur's right. The cultivated
zone is mainly in rice and sugar, boggy ground
which canalized the Japanese tanks along road lines
and brought them under the fire of American artillery. The heavily wooded character of the mountains did not permit the enemy to make full use
of his air force, and the familiarity of the Filipinos
on our side with every inch of the ground prevented attempts at infiltration.

Two massive assaults, one on the west coast and
one in the eastern zone, were broken up with heavy
casualties. General Homma of the Japanese forces
then brought up fresh troops and settled down to
a hammering campaign, designed to wear out the
defenders. MacArthur began to get into difficulties
about food, ammunition, and medical supplies.

Early in February the War Department ordered
him out of the Philippines and down to Australia

to take charge of the Allied Southwest Pacific Command. He escaped in a motor torpedo-boat, commanded by Lieutenant John D. Bulkeley, crawling by night among islands which were for the most part already in Japanese hands, and leaving the defense of Bataan in the hands of Lieutenant-General Jonathan Wainwright. The latter held out under daily attacks until April 8, his troops hoping against hope for relief, but on that day the accumulated shortages made it impossible to carry on. The peninsula was surrendered and a handful of American troops retired to the rock and tunnel fortress of Corregidor at the entrance of Manila Bay. The place stood through more than 260 air raids, but when the Japanese mounted heavy artillery on Mariveles Mountain and began to shell it at the end of April, the finish was in sight.

General Wainwright surrendered on May 6. Some 40,000 prisoners were taken there and on Bataan. They were treated with great barbarity; more than half of them died as the result of a long march under a hot sun without food or water or as the result of subsequent tortures in prison camps. They were the only fighting force in all the Indies that had paid for itself by the number of casualties it had inflicted.

CORREGIDOR flew the last American flag in the East. When the Japanese bombers made Manila Bay

untenable the American naval forces ran down to
Surabaya and fell under a joint command called
ABDA-flot (American-British-Dutch-Australian),
headed by Admiral Conrad Helfrich of the Dutch
Marine. He had two light cruisers, a flotilla leader
and six destroyers of his own, besides a number of
British ships, which, as they were mainly concerned
with the support of Singapore to the west, took
little part in the campaign; and a number of Dutch
submarines which aided the Americans in destruc-
tively raiding Japanese sea traffic and were the
most effective vessels of the combined squadron.

The ABDA-flot organization was set up on January 1, 1942; on the 11th the Japanese came down
with paratroops and landing forces at Tarakan in
Borneo and Menado at the tip of spidery Celebes
Island, taking both places easily and setting up air
strips to cover further advances.

They were impeded, but not very much, by the
operations of a handful of Dutch bombers and of
Patrol Wing 10, a formation composed of American
flying boats, which were such easy meat for the
swarms of Japanese fighters that they were known
as the "cold turkey squadron"; Macassar Strait,
where they principally operated, was known as
"turkey alley." Helfrich and those surrounding
him, fully realizing this was an air campaign,
cabled frantically for more planes, but the planes
were simply not in existence to send. On January

20 one of our submarines reported that a huge Japanese convoy was in Macassar Strait, obviously bound for Balikpapan, the biggest oil port of the region. Helfrich had the bulk of his little fleet out to the west covering convoys to Singapore, but he determined to try a night raid on this Japanese convoy and to rush the American light cruisers *Marblehead* and *Boise* up with four destroyers to make the raid on the night of the 23rd.

The operation began with misfortune. The *Boise* struck on an uncharted reef, ripped out part of her bottom, and was eliminated from the campaign. *Marblehead* had engine trouble, so the destroyers had to go in alone under Commander F. R. Talbot. At this time the Japanese were unable to operate their air scouts by night and Talbot kept his ships screened under the edge of the land during the day. He got right into the convoy as it lay off Balikpapan and four times marched back and forth among the crowded ships, firing torpedoes in both directions till the whole sea was ablaze. He escaped without losing a man, the first Allied victory of the war.

It did not halt the Japanese. By the beginning of February they had cleared all Malaya but Singapore Island itself, were in full possession of Balikpapan, and were so close to Amboina and Timor on the east that these places had to be abandoned without a fight. There was very little that could be done in the direction of Singapore, but Helfrich thought he might delay the Japanese advance at the center long enough to enable some air strength to reach him. He organized a striking force consisting of his own two cruisers, two American cruisers and eight destroyers, for a heavy raid up Macassar Strait against a Japanese convoy that was gathering at Balikpapan under escort of three cruisers and ten destroyers.

Under the flag of Rear-Admiral Karel Doorman of the Dutch navy the Allied force steamed out of Surabaya on February 3. Next morning it was caught near Bali by nearly 50 Japanese bombers. There was no air cover and the anti-aircraft artillery of the ships was primitive. Both *Houston* and *Marblehead* were badly hit, the former losing her after turret, the latter so damaged that she was barely kept afloat till she could reach Tjilitjap on the southern coast of Java for temporary repairs and then take the long route around the Cape of Good Hope for home. The Japanese got their convoy through to seize Macassar on Celebes Island, and on February 19 were ashore on Bali. Singapore had fallen four days before; Japanese planes were all over Java and the seas south of it, but a shipment of American fighter planes was reported on the way and Helfrich tried once more.

This time it was a daring night raid on the Japanese ships in harbor east of Java, made by succes-

sive waves of American destroyers following the
Dutch cruisers through the strait. The raid was a
success, the enemy losing a number of vessels; but it
did not drive him from Bali. Before the end of the
month the Japanese were massing heavy forces at
Bandjermasin north of the Java Sea for a landing
on Java itself. On the 26th their invasion convoy
put out from that port under heavy escort and
Doorman sailed to meet them. Some of the British
ships had fallen under his flag, but his losses had
been severe as the result of Japanese bombing raids
and all he could muster were two heavy cruisers,
one the still-damaged *Houston*, three light cruisers,
and ten destroyers.

They made contact with an enemy battle line
of considerably greater force near Bawean Island
on the afternoon of the 27th, and for a time there
was a gunnery action in which the Allied ships had
by no means the worst of it, driving two cruisers
from the enemy line with severe damage. But then
the British heavy cruiser *Exeter* was hit in the
engine room, dropped out, and Doorman's squadron was thrown into confusion. Japanese planes
kept dogging them in the twilight, Japanese ships
appearing and disappearing along the horizon. Our
side had lost two of its destroyers in the action; as
it fell dark one and then the other of the Dutch
cruisers suddenly blew up, apparently torpedoed
by submarines. The remaining vessels scattered.

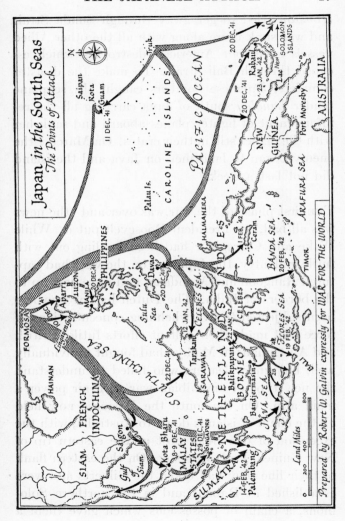

Japan in the South Seas
The Points of Attack

Prepared by Robert W. Galvin expressly for WAR FOR THE WORLD

Houston tried to get away through Sunda Strait
and was sunk there along with all the other Allied
vessels save four American destroyers which escaped through Bali Strait. To make the disaster
complete, Japanese bombers caught the seaplane
tender *Langley* south of Java carrying all the reinforcement of fighter planes aboard and sank her
with the planes still in their crates. On March 1 the
enemy began to land men on Java and the island
did not last a week.

THE first phase of the war was over and "the news
was all bad," as President Roosevelt put it. While
Wake and Corregidor had been holding out with
futile gallantry, the Japanese on the west had captured Rangoon and Mandalay and were now up to
the borders of India. The Dutch had everywhere
been subjected to overwhelming concentrations of
force that made their gallant efforts futile; British
and Australians in Malaya had fought individually
well, but under leaders who failed to understand
the new type of amphibian war with air power a
main arm. On the south the Japanese now held
all the chain of islands down to Australia, with the
exception of one small post at the eastern tip of
New Guinea, Port Moresby. On the eastern flank
of their line they had taken the Gilberts and were
established at Rabaul and in the northern Solomons, a chain of possessions which gave them a

vast triangular empire of sea and islands with its peak in the Kuriles. This empire was established by the middle of April, 1942. It contained all the supplies necessary to maintain war for the hundred years Japanese leaders foresaw it might last, and vast supplies of labor to exploit those resources.

The strategic sinew of that empire was the airplane. The first care of the invaders at every island was to set up air strips. They believed that when any point in their complex of islands was attacked the local defenses could instantly be supplemented from all the other bases within flight range, with a constant stream of planes being staged down from the homeland in the rear and still others hurried up by the forces afloat. They had demonstrated that planes could sink the heaviest ships in existence and that light ships were no match for an air attack. The outer chain of islands thus should be impenetrable in any practical sense, and behind that screen they could develop at their leisure the forces necessary to continue their conquest.

The news was indeed all bad. In February, German submarines in numbers were off the Atlantic coast and in the Caribbean. They sank ships on the very doorsills of the oil port of Aruba and in Chesapeake Bay. The Nazis had been turned back before Moscow, but the Russian army had been hit so hard that the Soviets were appealing for a landing in France at any cost to take some of the pres-

sure off them. England had barely escaped with
her life from the daylight bombings of 1940; now
every night the German bombers were over London, Coventry, Liverpool, Bristol. In Australia
the Japanense had struck at Port Darwin on the
northern coast with a crushing air raid on February 10, which smashed up all the shipping in the
harbor and so wrecked the place itself that we no
longer had a forward base from which the empire
could be attacked. Any strategic plans the United
States had were destroyed, and no new ones could
be developed in the face of the overwhelming necessities of defense.

CHAPTER II

MEN AND MATERIALS

DRAWING plans for possible wars is the province of the General Staff of the army and a similar organization with a somewhat different administrative setup in the navy. From early in 1940 on, it was clear to United States military leaders that the course on which the Nazis had embarked must sooner or later bring them into armed collision with the United States, save in the unlikely event of England defeating the Continental powers without help. It was in the military degree of probability that the Japanese and Italians would also be against us; accordingly, plans for such a war had been drawn. It is reasonable to assume that these were coördinated with British strategy at the secret conference in Argentia Bay in the summer of 1941, when Winston Churchill, President Roosevelt, and their leading military advisers met.

But in accordance with the traditions of American strategy and the fact that we had control of the sea, these plans were for an offensive war.

Mr. Churchill came to Washington in December, 1941, with the Chiefs of Staff of the British Army, Navy and Air Force, and a meeting was held with President Roosevelt, General Marshall, Admiral King, and General H. H. Arnold (of the United States Army Air Force). The Allied leaders were forced to take inventory and to make plans for a situation in which they were and would be for some time on the defensive, with no control of either sea or air in the Pacific and only a limited control of either against Germany.

The conference was so well agreed on the large lines of strategy that the obvious first step was to make it a permanent organization under the name of the Joint Chiefs of Staff. As the American material contribution was by far the greater and the determining factor in all operations, Washington was the seat of this body. The Russians were invited to join but refused, and throughout the war confined their participation to stating what they considered their requirements, material and strategic. The function of the Joint Chiefs of Staff, who met daily, was to decide the broad lines of strategy. President Roosevelt and Prime Minister Churchill laid down these lines in terms of policy—such as the decision to force the war in Europe to a conclusion before attacking Japan. The theater and force commanders, after the strategic decision had been taken, were then invited by the Chief of Staff most directly concerned to submit plans for operations.

Thus it might be held desirable by the two heads of state to launch a heavy blow against Italy and an operation that would force Japan to relax her preparations for moving on Australia. They would so inform the Chiefs of Staff. This body, after discussion, might report back that no major operation against Italy was possible with the forces available, but that a diversionary effort might profitably be undertaken in the Central Pacific. Admiral King would then notify Admiral Nimitz as Commander of the Pacific Fleet, and the latter's staff officers would draw a detailed plan, which would be examined at a conference between the two admirals in San Francisco. The plan, let us say, would involve the coöperation of a force of army heavy bombers and some British submarines. On his return to Washington with the detailed plan Admiral King would lay it before the Joint Chiefs of Staff. General Arnold would be asked to assign the bombers to Admiral Nimitz's operational control and the British naval representative would be asked to supply the submarines.

This is only a general outline; many variations arose in specific cases, and frequent disagreements occurred, as will appear in the course of the narrative. Mr. Churchill was an inveterate planner in his own right and the President had a proclivity for assuming control of everything on which he could lay his hands. That there were no worse effects than disagreement, that the organization on the whole worked more smoothly than any alliance known to history, was attributable on the one side to the fact that the Joint Chiefs of Staff held their meetings in Washington, out of Mr. Churchill's reach, and on the other side to the fact that Roosevelt was well served (and restricted) by General Marshall and Admiral King. Marshall was invincibly patient and persuasive; King, perhaps more than any other leader of the war, possessed a grasp of broad strategic principles and an inflexible determination not to be led from them into any side issues, however attractive. His contribution was an element of stability that nearly all committees of alliance in the past have lacked.

But this is looking into the future; for the present the most important facts before the Joint Chiefs of Staff were the resources with which they were to meet the double attack, so completely unprovoked that a considerable portion of the American press had been accusing the Administration of going out of its way to "appease" the Axis.

The British navy was entirely wedded to European waters and the campaign to keep Britain herself alive and operative as a base for aerial operations and for the eventual invasion of the Continent. It could give no help whatever in the Pacific, nor could its building yards, still under persistent air attack, do more than provide antisubmarine vessels at a rate that lagged slightly behind German U-boat production. Indeed, before the war the British had discovered not only devices that would detect any submarine under water but also depth charges that would destroy it; but the Germans had replied by building submarines in great quantity and by a refined operative technique which frequently permitted their captains to avoid attackers even after having been detected. A simple statistical fact makes the influence of numbers clear. Toward the close of World War I the Germans were able to keep at most 60 submarines at sea at one time, and these were hunted by over 700 Allied destroyers. After Pearl Harbor, the Germans were keeping well over 100 submarines at sea simultaneously, while the British had fewer than 200 destroyers and the American force in the Atlantic only about 100.

The technical advances in Diesel engines (which submarines use) had imposed further burdens on the defense. In World War I it was a comparatively poor craft that could not outrun a submarine, either for attack or defense. In World War II only a very good ship, powered by expensive and slowly built turbines, could keep up with the U-boats. The British had built large numbers of antisubmarine craft called corvettes, designed after fishing trawlers for rapid construction; but these were so slow that they could accomplish nothing against submarines save when the latter were submerged. The corvettes were accordingly forced at all times to remain close to the convoys they were protecting, making a purely passive defense.

The British army had lost practically all its equipment during the fall of France in 1940, and the demands upon it for the defense of Egypt were severe. Its resources of manpower were so limited that it could contemplate no grand strategy beyond furnishing a powerful wing to a force of Continental size fighting in Europe. This force must obviously come from the United States. But at the beginning of 1942, the time when the American army would be in a position to take the field with a force of Continental dimensions was still some distance in the future. The pre-war strength of the regular army had been comparable with that of the army of Paraguay. In the awakening after the fall of France in 1940, President Roosevelt secured the passage of a draft (Selective Service) act, and declaring a national emergency had called the National Guard into federal service and sent it to a series of camps, mainly in the South, for training in the new forms of war, about which no one in America yet knew more than very little.

This program was placed under Lieutenant-General Lesley McNair, and was extremely well conducted in the face of considerable obstacles, among which may be mentioned the fact that no active American officer had ever commanded as much as a division in the field, and that a typical National Guard formation arrived at its training camp with a full complement of polo ponies and four pianos, but with no trained cooks and no weapons. The shortage of equipment was, in fact, a serious question from the first. When the new army held maneuvers in Louisiana in 1941, tanks often had to be represented by trucks with "tank" lettered on their sides, and anti-aircraft guns were no more than logs mounted on pieces of board.

In one sense this was not altogether a disadvantage. The industrial machine had begun to swing toward war production in 1939 for the British and the French, and the process was accelerated in 1941 both by the involvement of Russia and rising fears that this country would be drawn in. The process took place late enough to permit much of the new equipment to be designed in the light of war experience, and to allow weapons, training methods, and organization to be made part of an integrated whole. It was decided from the beginning that in view of the necessity of supplying the Allies with material, the American population would not support an army larger than 100 field divisions strong (compared with Germany's 300 divisions). To give such an army the desired superiority at points of military contact and to make use of American mechanical aptitude and the American industrial plant, this force was mechanized to the last degree, especially with regard to its transportation equipment, a war of rapid movement being contemplated.

War experience had shown that continuous rapid movement, especially on roads, is unattainable without a fair command of the air. Moreover, the island of Britain offered an incomparable base for the operations of long-range bombers against the industrial machine supporting the Nazis. These reasons led to a concentration toward the air force, which became greater than that of any other nation in absolute numbers both of planes and men, and in proportion greater still. This dependence on the air arm was carried so far that heavy artillery was practically neglected.

Airplane production was from the beginning one of the key points of military industrial policy. The quantities turned out left little to be desired; and though the quality of the planes was severely criticized from time to time, no one can avoid the conclusion that on the whole American planes were the best in the war. We never had a short-range high-altitude fighter as good as the British Spitfire nor any plane with the maneuverability of the Japanese Zero; the British night bombers carried greater loads than any American plane. But our

long-range P-38 Lightning fighters, which could
serve equally well as light bombers, remained un-
matched by enemies or Allies till the Germans
brought out some of their jet planes at the very
end of the war. The P-47 Thunderbolt, heavy and
massive, proved incomparable for high-altitude
long-range work; and in all types of naval planes
American qualitative superiority was so marked
that all the Allies used practically nothing else.

All this, as well as the American bomber program which will be discussed later, was still in the
future when the Joint Chiefs of Staff held their first
meeting in Washington. A production rate of 10,000
planes a month was contemplated. The actual figure at that time was under 1,000 a month, and except for the naval planes and B-17 heavy bombers,
this production was largely of noncombat types
and planes not considered very satisfactory. The
draft process was stepped up and the training of
the new army speeded up, but it would be the
better part of the year before any considerable
force could either be trained or equipped.

Meanwhile, the war was in the hands of the navy.
This had been contemplated in our long-range
strategic planning, but not in the terms that faced
Admiral King when he took office. American naval
thought was offensive, and we found ourselves on
the defensive in both oceans. In the Pacific only
four battleships were available (soon to be joined

by a fifth from Pearl Harbor); the Japanese had twelve, and also at least nine carriers to bring against our six. They were, moreover, greatly favored by geography, for their early territorial seizures placed their fleet in direct contact with areas which produced all necessary supplies but ammunition.

Before the war it had been calculated that an American fleet operating in the western Pacific needed a paper strength of three ships for every two that could be put into action, the remaining third of our vessels being either en route homeward for supplies and repairs or on the way out after receiving these necessities. Sydney in Australia had a dockyard, and on the British flank of the empire seized by Japan there was another dockyard at Trincomalee in Ceylon, but neither could take care of anything larger than a light cruiser. Early in 1942 the British seized a base of sorts at Diego Suarez in Madagascar, but this action was taken to a great extent merely to keep the Japanese from gaining possession; the place had no spare parts or supplies that would serve Anglo-American ships. In a practical sense we were forced back to Mombasa on one flank of the new Japanese empire and to Pearl Harbor on the other.

A vast fleet had been laid down under the several programs for increasing the navy, but of the ships only three battleships, four light cruisers,

four anti-aircraft cruisers and some destroyers
would be ready in 1942, and these only at the very
end of the year. No other major reinforcement in
any class, and especially in the carrier class, could
be expected before the close of 1943. Indeed, this
was precisely one of the calculations that had led
the Japanese General Staff to make its attack at
this particular time. They were confident that
their blows at Pearl Harbor and in the Philippines
had paralyzed our striking forces for two years to
come; that in those two years they could so develop
the resources of the stolen Indies and so fortify
their positions there as to be beyond the power of
any attacking force that could reach them across
the distances of the Pacific, considering the difficulties under which the attackers would lie with
regard to supply, and the strength that could be
developed to oppose them in the form of island-
based air power.

When Mr. Churchill and Sir Alan Brooke, Chief
of the Imperial General Staff, embarked for Washington for another conference early in June, 1942,
there were still no data on which these assumptions
could be denied. In fact, the leading topic both
at this conference and the one succeeding it in
July, when General Marshall and Admiral King
when to London, was how to save Africa, where the
Germans had won a great victory. There was also
the question whether some diversionary effort

could not be undertaken to help the Russians, whose affairs were at a crisis with the Nazi drive to the Volga. It was decided that even were the Western Allies willing to sacrifice the men who would certainly be lost in a European landing with insufficient forces, the operation could not be undertaken. American troops were arriving weekly at bases set up in England and North Ireland, but most of them were neither fully trained nor equipped; their numbers were small in comparison to Continental armies; and, above all, ships were lacking in the form of landing craft to set them on the beaches of Europe.

CHAPTER III

THE CAMPAIGN OF THE CARRIERS

NEVERTHELESS, a few streaks of light illumined the horizon. On the shores of the Atlantic antisubmarine vessels were pouring from the yards, and the handful of blimps were proving unexpectedly potent as antisubmarine craft. In the Pacific, our admirals, who had always thought of sea power in terms of a line of battleships, had been forced by circumstance into a new type of naval war where the carrier was the capital ship.

The first tentative effort in this direction was made in December, 1941, when a carrier-and-cruiser force was pushed out to relieve Wake Island under Vice-Admiral W. S. Pye. Before they reached the place, word came from the island itself that major Japanese units were in the offing, and as no one cared to risk the last important units of the Pacific Fleet for so small an outpost, Pye's force turned back. While it was on the way at only eight knots, the carrier *Saratoga* was torpedoed by a Japanese submarine and sent to dock for months.

This miserable failure was profoundly unsatisfactory to the group of carrier admirals that included William F. Halsey, Frank Fletcher, Wilson Brown, and Aubrey Fitch. The next assignment was to open and keep open the supply lines to Australia and to get some troops into places like Samoa, New Caledonia, and the New Hebrides, which were not only valuable for themselves as sources of priceless alloy metals, but indispensable as bases and links for the island continent. These troop convoys were escorted only by destroyers; but out to the west of each, between it and the Japanese area, ran one of the carrier task forces, composed of a group of cruisers with a carrier at the center, an idea new in war.

By mid-January it had become probable that the next step in the Japanese career of empire-building would be outward from the southeastern angle of their holdings toward the islands that linked with Australia. The carrier men thought they could discount such a move by employing the occasion of their passage through the area for a heavy raid on the harbors of the Gilberts and Marshalls, where the ships of the enemy's invasion convoy must perforce gather. Admiral Nimitz, as fleet commander, accepted the heavy responsibility of allowing them to try it with the only real naval force we had in the Pacific at the time. The raid fell on February 1, 1942. Halsey with one carrier task force attacked Kwajalein, Wotje, and Maloe-lap in the Marshalls, while Fletcher with another group fell on the Gilberts. Both successfully evaded enemy scouts by running fast through the night and flying off planes to strike just at dawn. The cruisers ran in under the air attack to subject the objectives to shell fire. The attack was a complete success, our loss was insignificant (with only one ship hit and 14 planes lost) and the Japanese loss very heavy, some 73,000 tons of shipping being destroyed and the local air groups in the assaulted islands being virtually wiped out.

Halsey was therefore allowed to try it again, this time against Wake Island, which the Japanese had been turning into a forward air base of considerable importance, and Marcus Island, which had been a Japanese possession for half a century. Wake was struck on February 24. Halsey's group then pushed on to strike Marcus on March 4 without returning to base, and once again his success was complete, with no damage to the ships but with the Japanese installations pretty well cut to pieces.

The fact that fast-moving carriers, able to escape enemy interference by the use of their own planes for scouting, could so closely approach the seats of Japanese power led directly to the most spectacular event of the early war. The new carrier *Hornet* had been on her shakedown cruise in the Caribbean.

She was now brought to San Francisco, where in great secrecy she took on a squadron of 16 army two-motored B-25 bombers under Colonel James H. Doolittle. (It is significant of the state of preparation at the time that this was the only squadron of thoroughly trained and experienced B-25 pilots that the army had.) Two-motored planes had never been flown from a ship before; these were specially altered for the purpose and their pilots specially trained. At sea, *Hornet* was joined by the carrier *Enterprise,* flying Admiral Halsey's flag, which was to furnish air cover and scouting for the operation. The fleet ran through high latitudes at speed and on April 18, 700 miles from the Japanese islands, launched its bombers in a raid across Tokyo which caused considerable destruction and something like a long-term panic in the Japanese capital, and corresponding elation in Allied circles. The bombers flew on toward prepared bases in China. There all were wrecked, as they had been forced to take off from the ship some hours earlier than originally planned when Halsey's squadron encountered a cordon of Japanese fishing boats on patrol.

This concluded the period of the raids. The direct damage inflicted was small in proportion to the scale of the war, but the losses suffered were altogether negligible and the carrier task forces had demonstrated not only their ability to take care of themselves without heavy gunnery support but also their ability to achieve surprise, the most important single element in offensive war. They had also—and this is perhaps the direction in which the carrier raids told most heavily in the total history of the war—introduced into the counsels of Japan an element of doubt as to the validity of the whole Japanese system of imperial defense by air from island fields.

For the time being this remained a cause without an effect. The Japanese were sweeping on to round out their imperial domain on the southeast and the bulk of their forces afloat were concentrated in that region. They had seized the big harbor of Rabaul in New Britain and rapidly erected it into a place of arms second only to their long-held base at Truk. Early in February, 1942, they took Lae and Salamaua on the north coast of New Guinea and began to work small outposts along that shore eastward, preparatory to crossing the precipitous, jungle-covered Owen Stanley Mountains for an attack on Port Moresby. The headquarters view at this time was that Moresby could not be held, which would mean the invasion of Australia, and it seemed confirmed by minor defeats inflicted on the slender Australian forces by trained Japanese jungle fighters among the mountains.

Nevertheless, there was no use giving up so valuable a spot without an effort, and during February Rear-Admiral Wilson Brown was sent south with a task force built around the giant carrier *Lexington* to see what he could accomplish against Rabaul, which our scout planes had reported as crowded with enemy shipping. As Brown's force was running north of the Solomons toward Rabaul it was detected by Japanese scouts (February 20) and shortly after attacked by two formations of heavy land-based bombers. This made Brown's mission a failure (there was no use going on with all chances of surprise eliminated), but the *Lexington* fighter patrols shot down all but one of the attacking Japanese, the big carrier was undamaged, and our officers learned the encouraging fact that American carriers need not avoid areas where they would be under air attack—something that had been notably untrue of carriers in the war up to this time.

This led to the decision to make a serious air attack on the Japanese at Lae and Salamaua. The carrier *Yorktown,* originally scheduled to go with Halsey to Wake, was sent down to join Brôwn's force. Two ships with their escorts made a fast run up Coral Sea to the neighborhood of Moresby and launched their planes across the mountains at daybreak on March 10. It was the heaviest raid yet flown from carriers, and the planes had the luck to catch one big convoy unloading, with another coming in. Surprise was complete and both convoys were nearly wiped out at a cost of only one plane to ourselves.

This raid had important effects. One was the decision to cling to Port Moresby and defend Australia from there. The Japanese attempted to press through the narrow pass in the mountains but the loss of the two convoys had fatally disrupted their supply organization and their advance was brought to a halt.

They had now cleaned up everything in the Indies to the westward except for some guerrilla operations in the Philippines, and they determined to use their major forces for the type of operation that had thus far served them so well. An invasion force of transports with seaplane tenders and supplies was sent down to establish a base among the Louisiades off the eastern end of New Guinea, to pinch out Moresby. Another force of the same kind went down to establish a base at Guadalcanal and Tulagi in the southern Solomons as a preliminary toward advancing on New Caledonia.

The Japanese had attributed the Lae-Salamaua attack to Australian land-based bombers. To prevent a repetition of this affair, they supported their convoy for the Louisiades with a squadron consisting of two carriers with cruiser and destroyer escort. (C on map on page 42.) Some Allied ships would be operating in the Coral Sea; to prevent any interference from this quarter and at the same time to cut off anything that might come up from the New Hebrides or New Caledonia, a major battle fleet swept down from Truk. It contained at least two carriers with several heavy cruisers which could keep pace with them. (D on map on page 42.) Its line of advance carried it southeast around the Solomons and so into Coral Sea, much as our own carrier forces had formed their moving screen for the advance of our forces to Australia.

This movement was timed for early May. Almost as soon as it started, our high command had knowledge of at least the invasion fleets, through submarine scouting and broken code messages. Halsey was far in the north Pacific, returning from the Tokyo raid, and could not possibly reach the scene of action in time. The burden had to be carried by the *Lexington-Yorktown* carrier force, now under command of Vice-Admiral Frank Fletcher. He had been in the Samoa area, keeping well clear of Australia to avoid discovery by Japanese planes. As the two enemy invasion forces came down he rushed west, then north up to Coral Sea to a position just south of Guadalcanal before daybreak on May 4. With *Lexington* out to the south, furnishing air guard against any enemy vessels that might approach from that direction, *Yorktown's* planes were shot over the island on to the enemy shipping crowded in Tulagi harbor. Once more surprise was complete; the whole Japanese convoy and its escort were simply butchered, at least 12 of the 15 ships being sent down at once. (1 and B on map on page 42.)

As soon as his planes returned, Fletcher ran rapidly westward in an effort to catch the other Japanese invasion fleet among the Louisiades. This enemy group does not seem to have put its base-builders ashore, as it had been attacked by some planes from Australia on the 4th. The Japanese Admiral had called in his supporting carrier task group for help against the Australian flyers, as well as against some cruisers from the MacArthur command which the Japanese scouts had found maneuvering up toward the region of Port Moresby. The Japanese carrier task group accordingly hurried on that night, the night of the 4th, toward daybreak one carrier and her escorts were dispatched westward, while the other ran south through the island passes toward Coral Sea.

It was this second carrier, *Shoho*, the newest in the Japanese navy, that Fletcher's scouts discovered when they went out on their dawn patrol next morning. His attack groups had already warmed up; they took off at once, caught *Shoho* just turning into the wind to launch planes and destroyed her in five minutes with ten heavy bomb hits and fifteen torpedoes. That broke the hearts of the Japanese western forces both of invasion and support; they abandoned the project of setting up a base

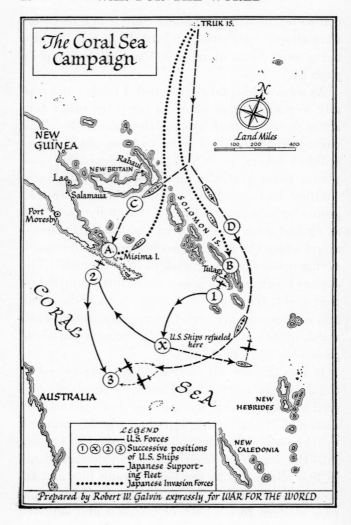

The Coral Sea Campaign

Prepared by Robert W. Galvin expressly for WAR FOR THE WORLD

and steamed away north, fearful that Fletcher would hit them again. (2 and A on map.)

But Fletcher was not thinking of hitting them again. While his planes were in the air he had received a message from the tanker *Neosho*, which had refueled him during the night and was now making eastward toward Samoa under guard of a single destroyer. She was being heavily attacked by carrier-type planes. The destroyer had already gone down—and presently there were no more messages, which meant the tanker was gone too. It was the American Admiral's first intimation of the presence of a second enemy supporting fleet, the big one with the battleships in it. This fleet was coming along a line that would pin Fletcher back into the desolate bight between Australia and New Guinea. He turned south, running all day parallel to the coast of the Continent to gain room, but that night the Japanese scouts found him, and when dawn made air operations possible, the weather was all in their favor, for over our ships it was bright and clear while over theirs, the clouds made good cover.

Fletcher's scouts discovered them nevertheless. Attack groups from the two fleets crossed each other and there was violent fighting in the air and on the sea that lasted all morning long. *Yorktown* got a bomb hit through her flight deck that killed some 44 men, but the enemy concentrated chiefly on the larger *Lexington* and hit her with no less than five torpedoes. The damage-control men got the ship to an even keel and put out all the fires but one; toward evening that one reached the gasoline system. The big carrier blew out her sides and had to be abandoned. The Japanese did not know this; they had no planes left to scout with, for nearly all had been shot down in the air combat and those that remained went into the sea because the decks of both their carriers had been ripped up by our air groups. Like the western, their eastern fleet turned and ran for home. (3 on map.)

This was the Battle of Coral Sea, a three-day battle, the first of its kind in history, in which no ship sighted an enemy vessel. It saved—what? Probably Australia, where both the local forces and our own were still of the most exiguous order, and there are few good positions for military defense; certainly the lifeline to Australia, for the New Hebrides lie within easy reach of Guadalcanal, where the Japanese had tried to set up a base. Materially, Coral Sea was not much better than a drawn battle, but it gave the Japanese imperial program its first check and that check was a severe one.

THERE is reason to believe that the enemy had planned his offensive in the north sometime before. The defeat at Coral Sea, however, undoubtedly forced him to hurry it on without waiting for attrition further to cut down the strength of the American fleet. Until Pearl Harbor was rendered useless as an operating base for our navy, there was little chance that the Japanese could round out the vital and vulnerable southeastern corner of their empire without interference from our heavy forces. The whole Japanese system of war was one of playing such forces out of position rather than attempting to fight them down in pitched battle, which involved an amount of attrition that their own more slender resources did not permit them to accept. It is also likely that they believed our attention was now firmly fixed to the southward and that the bulk of our sea strength was concentrated in that direction for the support of the Australian lifeline. That is, their intelligence service, so superbly conducted at the beginning of the war, was now at fault.

Not so the parallel American organization. As early as the late weeks of May, Admiral Nimitz knew from deciphered code messages that shortly after the first of June, 1942, the Japanese would approach the Aleutian chain with a task group woven around two small carriers, and if events were propitious would attempt to affect a lodgment near Dutch Harbor on Unalaska Island. At the same time three fleets would attack Midway Island, outpost of the Hawaiian chain. One would be a striking force consisting of two battleships and four big carriers with supporting cruisers and destroyers; the second, a support force of two more battleships with heavy cruisers and destroyers; the third, an invasion force with at least 14 big transports, as many supply vessels, four more heavy cruisers, destroyers and submarines. With Midway gained, they could render Pearl Harbor nearly useless as a base by continual air raids; and if things went well could get a grip on one of the Hawaiian Islands. Nimitz instantly began a counterconcentration.

The army diverted a number of heavy Flying Fortress bombers that had been destined for Europe, sending them out to Hawaii at once. A fleet of our battleships, old and slow, but unequaled in armor and gunpower, was rushed out from San Francisco to the area north and west of Hawaii. The carriers *Enterprise* and *Hornet* with their retinue of cruisers put to sea and were shoved into position just east of Midway, where they were presently joined by *Yorktown*, which came at speed all the way from Coral Sea with workmen repairing her bomb hit from that action. Every Marine fighter plane that could be assembled was rushed out to Midway. Halsey was ill; the carriers were under Vice-Admiral Raymond A. Spruance, who had commanded the cruisers during the raid, the very antithesis of Halsey as a leader, a cold, severe, passionless intellectual known in the fleet as "the human machine."

The Japanese attack opened June 3 at Dutch Harbor, when some planes came through the mist that perpetually hangs around that place and dropped their bombs without much effect. The fogs closed in solidly after that first attack (we lost several of the big PBY patrol planes which went out in that murk to hunt the enemy), and it was next morning before it was clear enough to let the Japanese commander launch planes again. Before he could do so, he was set upon by a squadron of Army P-40s escorting a group of fast twin-motored bombers. The commander of the Japanese expedition could have expected to be counter-attacked, but what completely upset his equilibrium was that the attack came from his rear, back toward Japan where, according to his best information, no important American base lay. He checked by means of his scout planes, losing considerably in the process, and found that our engineers had indeed set up a secret base on Umnak Island, well out in the Aleutian chain, now swarming with fast fighters and still faster bombers. The Japanese incontinently gave up his part of the operation.

Days later his ships reached Attu, Agattu, and Kiska, the uninhabited outermost islands of the Aleutian group. He put his occupation forces ashore and they began to develop the islands as a minor base.

Three hours after the first flashing contact at Dutch Harbor, a patrol plane found the Japanese invasion force coming in on Midway 700 miles slightly south of west from that island. It was too far for a normal air strike to fly but in the dark hours of the night four other patrol planes took torpedoes out to try a blow at the enemy. They hit two transports and sent one down.

The real battle did not begin till next morning when, just after dawn, another patrol plane found the Japanese striking force under the clouds of a weather front northwest of Midway. The enemy carriers had just launched their planes; in the air they crossed all the land-based bombers of Midway coming out for the counterattack and the warning was sufficient to get the Marine fighters at the island into the air. The air fighting at the island was furious; it cost the Japanese 45 bombers and us most of the defending fighters, with considerable damage to gun emplacements and an oil tank set afire. But in the counterattack at least one and possibly two of the Japanese carriers were hit, together with several other ships, and at about 9:00 o'clock the enemy commander swung back to the northwest to refuel and rearm his aircraft, apparently no little surprised at the vigor of the reception he had encountered.

Spruance and his carriers had been well out to the eastward to avoid observation. Now his planes came into action, a complete and horrifying surprise to the enemy. At Coral Sea our torpedo planes had done the severest damage; now what air patrols the Japanese had up were concentrated at the low levels where torpedo-carriers operate and shot down all but six of the 41 Americans in the attack. But this left our dive bombers free and they fell on the enemy carriers. Before noon three of them were burning furiously, the two battleships were afire, and at least one destroyer had gone down.

The Japanese carrier *Hiryu* escaped under some clouds off to the north. Her planes traced Spruance's formation as it swung back toward Midway to avoid contact with the Japanese heavy gunnery ships. A little after noon, Japanese planes struck the carrier *Yorktown* and damaged her severely, but in the counterattack all our air groups got in on *Hiryu* and sank her. This delayed matters so much that no further attack on the main Japanese fleet was possible that evening; Spruance did not know that, as night closed in, *Soryu* and *Akagi*, the burning Japanese carriers, had sunk without further strikes from our forces and the carrier *Kaga* had been sent down by the submarine *Nautilus*, which had just reached the scene.

By daybreak of the 5th the absence of Japanese

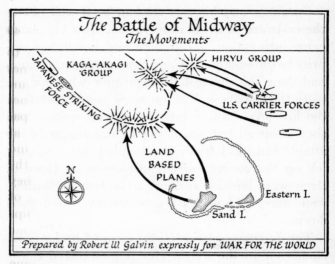

The Battle of Midway
The Movements

Prepared by Robert W. Galvin expressly for WAR FOR THE WORLD

planes and the fact that the remaining ships were in full retreat made it clear that something very serious had happened to the enemy carriers. Leaving the crippled *Yorktown* behind, Spruance flung himself into the pursuit with his other two carriers. They caught nothing that day and *Yorktown*, together with a destroyer, was sunk by a Japanese submarine, but Flying Fortresses from Hawaii damaged some of the routed enemy ships. On the morning of the 6th, Spruance's fliers did catch up with the disorganized foe and in an attack which met no aerial opposition sent two destroyers and the heavy cruiser *Mikuma* to the bottom and battered another heavy cruiser so badly that she had to be completely rebuilt and was not seen again for nearly two years.

No battle but the final one can be called fully decisive, yet Midway decided much. The salvation of that island and of Hawaii behind it was only the most obvious of its effects. It dealt a deadly blow to Japanese command morale, destroying much of their offensive spirit, for no Japanese fleet in history had ever taken such a defeat. It finished the account of the Japanese air service begun at Coral Sea, debarring them from any broad oceanic operations till their losses were made good. It took nearly all of their relatively few highly trained and skillful carrier pilots; the four carriers that went down were the only flight decks they had left in action with the exception of the light carriers that had been in the Aleutian raid. Moreover, it threw the whole war into a domain for which the Japanese had made no plan, and before they could work one out they were forced to adjust their plans to those of their opponents. The tide that had flowed over nearly a sixth of the earth's surface and nearly a quarter of its population reached its highwater mark at Midway and from that point ebbed.

CHAPTER IV

GUADALCANAL

ADMIRALS King and Nimitz were now faced with a difficult decision. The victory at Midway in June, 1942, was decisive, but the decision was conditional. Unless the Japanese were counter-attacked at once and were thus forced to use their resources for purposes primarily defensive, they would be able to rebuild the mobile striking force that centered around their carriers and was closely interlocked with the land-based air power of their island strips; they could then themselves attack again toward Australia and the southeast. An abrupt increase of enemy submarine activity in this area indicated that such might be their purpose. On the other hand, the decision to invade French North Africa had already been taken. This blow would require all the resources of the Western Allies, particularly in trained troops and shipping. The German submarine campaign in the North Atlantic had already cut so deeply into merchant tonnage that Admiral Nimitz was informed he

The Southern Solomons

Land Miles

0 25 50 100

SANTA ISABEL

Ramos I.

Russell Is.

Cape Esperance

Savo I.

Tulagi

Florida I.

Indispensable Strait

Auki

MALAITA

Su'u

Deep Bay

MARAMASIKE

Lunga

HENDERSON FIELD

Aola

Saa

Wanderer Bay

Ullawa I.

Bolonda

GUADALCANAL

Cape Recherche

SAN CRISTÓBAL

Olu Malau Is.

Kira Kira

SOLOMON SEA

Cape Surville

Bellona I.

RENNELL I.

NEW GUINEA

Rabaul

Lae

NEW BRITAIN

SOLOMON ISLANDS

Port Moresby

Milne Bay

Cape York

CORAL SEA

AUSTRALIA

Land Miles

100 200 400

Prepared by Robert W. Galvin expressly for WAR FOR THE WORLD

would have to conduct his operations with one-fifth less shipping than he had possessed during the strictly defensive phase just terminated.

The spot chosen for the first American offensive of the war must thus be at once one where the Japanese were so deeply committed that they would feel a defense necessary; one that could be taken with limited forces, and one that could be readily supported from Allied bases so near at hand that much shipping was not needed. These three conditions were met by the Guadalcanal-Tulagi complex in the Southern Solomons, the outermost angle of Japanese empire. An additional argument in favor of selecting this area was that after the disaster inflicted upon them in the first phases of the Coral Sea battle, the Japanese had again infiltrated the place and were setting up an airfield on Guadalcanal. If it became operative, their bombers could render unsafe the harbors of the New Hebrides, New Caledonia, and, indeed, the whole communications link with Australia.

The operation as a whole was placed under the direction of Vice-Admiral R. L. Ghormley, who had been in command of the South Pacific area since April. To him were assigned all the available carriers (three), one new battleship, all the cruisers not needed in European waters or for keeping watch on the new Japanese outposts in the Aleutians, and most of the vessels attached to General

MacArthur's Southwest Pacific Command. The First Marine Division was to be a landing force. Meanwhile, the old battleships, with one of the escort carriers converted from a merchant hull, remained off San Francisco in case the Japanese should attempt a counterattack with their remaining ships.

New Zealand was the assembly point for the expedition. It reached the region of Guadalcanal at dawn on August 7 and, under a screen of carrier planes that drove everything Japanese from the sky, put its troops ashore. On Guadalcanal itself the early opposition was smothered by the fire of the ships, the beachhead was secured early, and by the second morning the nearly completed airfield was in American hands. Tulagi, where the harbor lay, proved a tougher nut. Both on the island of that name and on smaller ones commanding the bay, the Japanese had dug themselves into complex limestone caves from which they kept up so accurate a fire that little progress was made by evening and our casualties were heavy. During the night they counterattacked; it was noon of the 8th before the position was won.

Admiral Fletcher, in charge of the fleet, drew his carriers out southward during the night to keep them clear of Japanese air attacks, which were begun on the afternoon of the 7th and continued through the next and many other days by Japanese bombers staged down through the Upper Solomons from Rabaul. During the night the sea approaches to the position were covered by a squadron of four American and two Australian heavy cruisers with some destroyers, under Rear-Admiral V. A. C. Crutchley, operating in the lagoon which is bisected by Savo Island. He had nowhere near enough destroyers—too many were needed in the Atlantic to fight off German submarines—and the men on all the ships were at the last point of fatigue, having been kept at their stations for 72 hours by the Japanese air attacks and the night fighting on Tulagi which they had been supporting. On the night of the 8th the men were allowed to take some rest.

The moment proved ill-chosen. At 1:30 in the morning a squadron of fast Japanese cruisers and destroyers that had escaped our scouts by running close along the shores of the upper islands came dashing around the south flank of Savo. They were right on top of our ships, firing with gun and torpedo, before any alarm could be given, and were out and away before effective counteraction could be taken. Behind they left destruction. The American heavy cruiser *Quincy* blew up on the spot; before dawn *Astoria* and *Vincennes* with the *Canberra* had gone down, *Chicago* had a torpedo hole that would keep her in dock for many months, and two of our destroyers were badly damaged. It was an appalling defeat; far worse, because of the surrounding circumstances, than Pearl Harbor. Morale in the fleet was considerably shaken and so was public confidence in the navy when two months later news of the losses was allowed to come out.

At Guadalcanal itself the covering force had been destroyed. The cargo ships that were unloading supplies for the Marines on the island had to steam away with their cargoes still aboard and the Japanese there promptly rallied to begin a long series of attacks against our beachhead. The beachhead itself consisted only of a small perimeter around the airfield. The Marines quickly ran short of ammunition and for a long time had to live on captured Japanese rice. Day and night they were bombarded by Japanese planes, and when the enemy discovered that our ships had left the lagoon they also brought surface vessels down to shell the lines.

Within ten days the enemy began landing reinforcements on the island, bringing them in by night aboard fast transports which could make the run under cover of dark from a point too far north to be attacked during daylight by planes from our carriers. The Marines managed to beat off all attacks, the supply situation gradually improved as occasional fast transports ran in, and on August 20 the air strip on Guadalcanal was in condition to receive some planes.

WE had only a handful (planes were still a major shortage in all combat areas), but their arrival inaugurated a period and style of warfare that was to endure for more than a year from the middle of 1942. The essential element of this fighting was violent and continual crossraiding between Japanese planes based on the upper islands and our own from Guadalcanal field. The favorite targets on both sides were the supply ships that served the installation and the light warships that protected the carriers.

On land the Japanese probably suffered less from these bombings than our forces, being more adept both at concealment and at putting their essential installations underground. At sea and in the almost continuous air fighting which accompanied the raids their losses were much the heavier, the plane losses stabilizing at the astonishing figure of five or six to one. The reasons were twofold. Japanese technicians had made the mistake of providing a type of plane which, while very fast and more maneuverable than the American machines, was unarmored and lightly built, so that it blew up or crashed as the result of injuries which would not even put an American machine out of action.

Their naval air service—the planes that operated from land bases in the Solomons belonged to that service—had never recovered from the cruel loss in experienced pilots suffered at Coral Sea and

Midway. The men who replaced those pilots were by no means their equals, while our new pilots were of high quality. The result was that the deterioration throughout the Japanese naval air service became progressive. With some effort the Japanese industrial system managed to replace the mechanical losses, but the proportion of capable flight personnel in the operating areas showed a steady decline.

These effects, however, became perceptible only over a long period. At the end of August the situation of the Marines on Guadalcanal was not far from desperate. The same day their first planes arrived at the island a Japanese group, which had landed east of the airfield, joined another from the opposite direction in a coördinated attack that was beaten off only with difficulty; while simultaneously word was received from submarines and radio intercepts that a powerful fleet was coming down from Truk and the enemy air forces in the Upper Solomons had been heavily reinforced.

The Japanese were evidently preparing a general air-sea-land offensive to recapture the island. Rear-Admiral Thomas C. Kinkaid came up from the south to meet them with a fleet at whose core were the carriers *Saratoga* and *Enterprise* and the new battleship *North Carolina*. The Japanese were much stronger on the surface and had the support of numerous land-based planes, but their air groups were relatively untrained. The fleets made contact on August 24 when our ships were off the Eastern Solomons, from which the battle takes its name. It was another of those mutual attacks from the air like Coral Sea and Midway. *Enterprise* was badly damaged by bombs, but the enemy lost the carrier *Ryujyo*, had a transport and some small vessels sunk, and were completely stripped of air cover. Their major surface vessels, mostly damaged, dared not press home in the face of the plane strength we still had, and the expedition turned back.

Meanwhile, the enemy had remarked our unwillingness to trust surface vessels in the waters around Guadalcanal by night since the disaster at Savo Island. They had therefore built up a new system that became known as the "Tokyo Express." It was a development of the emergency method by which their first reinforcements had been sent in. Squadrons of cruisers and destroyers assembled in the area of the Shortland Islands, just beyond the range of our light bombers. (Only a few of the heavy B-17 Flying Fortresses were in the area and they were generally ineffective against mobile targets.) As soon as twilight put an end to American aerial operations, these Japanese squadrons would run down "the Slot" between the double line of the Solomons at full speed, arriving off Guadalcanal about midnight. While part of the squadron landed its troops on the western, Japanese-held end of the island, the remainder pushed on to shell the American positions. Then the whole group generally circled Savo to make the return trip.

Before the end of September they had thus succeeded in getting an entire new division into Guadalcanal, and twice their flotillas succeeded in catching and destroying light American vessels similarly engaged in bringing support to the Marines. On September 14 the enemy launched an attack along the ground that succeeded in making the Guadalcanal airfield temporarily useless by placing it under artillery fire. This represented the most serious crisis yet to occur in the campaign, for the same day the navy lost one of its few remaining carriers, *Wasp*. She had been operating, as the custom then was, south of the Solomons, patroling a rather narrow area and lending the support of her planes to Guadalcanal. The Japanese observed the regularity of the procedure and laid a submarine trap. In a single afternoon they not only sank the carrier but also a destroyer and secured a torpedo hit on the battleship *North Carolina* which sent her in for repairs. The convoy this force had been covering, however, made Guadalcanal safely, unloaded reinforcements by daylight, and the Marines were able to drive the Japanese back from the airfield.

The loss of the *Wasp* brought about the supersession of Admiral Ghormley by Admiral Halsey, whose great popularity in the fleet caused an immediate elevation of its morale, and whose arrival in the South Pacific was signalized by another event of great importance. On October 11 scouting aircraft had detected a Tokyo Express among the Western Solomons; not only cruisers and destroyers but a number of large and fast transports, indicating an effort on the part of the enemy to land major reinforcements.

After dark a squadron of four American cruisers under Rear-Admiral Norman Scott slipped up to the region of Cape Esperance at the western end of Guadalcanal. They arrived ahead of the Japanese and by means of radar "saw" the latter coming in before they themselves were detected—the first occasion when the new device had been so employed. The enemy were completely surprised and caught out of position as our ships opened fire. In an action that lasted not quite half an hour the Japanese lost one of their heavy cruisers and two flotilla leaders, beside several of the loaded transports. A single destroyer was lost on our side. It was the first time in the war that American surface ships had won a battle, and the victory was crushing. In that part of the navy, Cape Esperance rather than Midway has always been regarded as the turning point of the war.

THE battle also had another permanent effect. It convinced the Japanese that Guadalcanal could be regained only by a major effort. They continued to run their Tokyo Express throughout the middle of October, 1942, but the garrison around Henderson Field (as it had been named) had now been reinforced by nearly a full division of American army troops. It was a division made up of scattered units, called the Americal, bearing no number and under command of Major-General A. M. Patch.

These units were intended to relieve the Marines, who were showing evident fatigue; they arrived just in time to meet one of the most determined ground assaults the Japanese as yet launched, and on October 24 the Marines had to be put back in to rescue the less experienced infantry. For a time it was doubtful whether the field could be held, the enemy having infiltrated so heavily that the whole jungle battlefield was in inextricable confusion. All the planes on the field were destroyed by shelling. But the American artillery was so effective that the Japanese could work up no concentration strong enough to drive home their attack, and by the evening of October 26 our forces had beaten it off and were moving slowly forward.

By this time the fleets had again been in action. The Japanese attack on land was only part of a general power drive to break the American forces. The 24th, which saw the beginning of their movement on the ground, also brought the heaviest raid they had yet launched from airfields in the Upper Solomons, a raid which succeeded in disabling many of our planes. On the morning of the 26th scouting aircraft found another major Japanese fleet coming down from Truk. It was organized in three groups, operating at some distance from each other in accordance with the usual Japanese practice. One was a battleship group, centered around two of these craft, apparently intended to finish off cripples or to run in and shell the American positions on the island. The other two were built around carriers, the big *Shokaku* and *Zuikaku* (now repaired after the damage they had suffered in the Coral Sea), one of them supported by a new light carrier.

The American forces were similarly organized in groups around carriers. There were only two of these, *Enterprise* and *Hornet* (*Saratoga* had again taken a submarine torpedo on August 21 and was still under repair). But a radical difference existed between this American fleet and the one that went up to Midway. Each of the carrier groups here contained one of the new anti-aircraft cruisers and each contained one of the new fast battleships. One of the latter, *South Dakota*, had injured her bottom on an uncharted reef and had returned to

Pearl Harbor for repairs. There she had received the full equipment of over 100 of the new 40 and 20 millimeter automatic anti-aircraft guns, the first vessel to be armed with a multiplicity of these weapons.

Both these groups were operating near the Santa Cruz Islands on the morning of the 26th when contact was made. Our ships were in clear weather and the enemy under a fog front, so that the Japanese got their attack groups into the air first. The battle turned into one more of those double sea-air engagements. The Japanese concentrated on *Hornet* in their first attacks and hit her so heavily that she lost all power and was set afire. An effort was made to tow her out, but it failed when the towing cable snapped during a second air attack; she had to be scuttled. The case of *Enterprise* was different. She was defended by *South Dakota* and with the help of the battleship's guns cut the attackers to pieces, though they appeared in a concentration far heavier than any yet made against an American ship.

Meanwhile, our own attack groups had gone in on the various enemy squadrons. Their light carrier had been damaged earlier by one of our patrol planes and turned out of action. Now both *Shokaku* and *Zuikaku* were heavily hit by the dive bombers and their decks so ripped open that they could not handle planes. Several of the Japanese major gun-

nery ships were hurt, including both the battleships, and one of their cruisers was sunk. Toward
evening both fleets turned away from further contact.

The Battle of Santa Cruz was counted as something like a defeat by our command at the time,
since we had lost a destroyer in addition to *Hornet*,
but its effects were those of a victory. The lost carrier's planes landed on Guadalcanal and furnished
just in time the air support that had been lost
with the destruction of the planes at the field; and
though we were now down to a single, damaged,
carrier, the battle struck the death knell of the
Japanese carrier service. Over a hundred of their
planes had been shot down (56 by the improved
automatic weapons), and of the remainder both
planes and pilots were lost in most instances
through lack of decks on which to land. The enemy
decided they could not afford to accept further sea-
air battles on any terms and never again attempted
it. Moreover, the losses in their carrier groups
caused a change in their naval policy which fundamentally affected the whole war. They had laid
down six new battle cruisers, two battleships, and
several other major units. The battleships and battle cruisers were now altered to new carriers, and
all the rest of the Japanese shipbuilding program
was pinched to provide the necessary materials for
these vessels.

THE one Japanese effort that had not failed was the running of the Tokyo Express. It exercised a control of the waters around Guadalcanal by night in the fall of 1942 that was hampered only by the operations of a squadron of newly arrived American motor torpedo-boats (PTs). A week after the Battle of Santa Cruz the Japanese again landed a force east of the airfield to attempt a new pincers movement. But the experienced pilots from *Enterprise* had now joined those of *Hornet* as the air garrison of the field and they provided sufficient cover to permit light American forces to operate at will in the lagoon by daylight. Our cruisers and destroyers shelled the Japanese flanking force so heavily that it lost all its supplies, broke up under an attack by the Marines, and was driven back into the central hills to be there exterminated.

Our forces also had the advantage that planes from MacArthur's Southwest Pacific Command could scout the enemy concentration point of Rabaul. Early in November the Japanese began to assemble in that area and it was evident that another effort to throw heavy forces into Guadalcanal was imminent, though on different terms from that which had failed at Santa Cruz. By November 11 they had four battleships in the area with numerous cruisers, about thirty destroyers and enough transports to contain two divisions of troops. They clearly intended to trump the cruiser and destroyer forces, so effective at Cape Esperance, by putting in ships of the first line, and to knock out our planes on the ground by night shelling as they had temporarily succeeded in doing during October.

A large American convoy of troops and supplies reached Guadalcanal on November 12, escorted by five cruisers and eight destroyers under Rear-Admiral D. J. Callaghan. About noon, as the ships were unloading, 32 Japanese torpedo planes suddenly shot low over Florida Island upon them, the first wave of the grand attack in what was intended to be a surprise. But it was no surprise; a radar station had given adequate warning, the American fighters were up to hit the Japanese planes as they came in, and the fire from the ships, particularly the new anti-aircraft cruiser *Atlanta*, was deadly beyond expectation. Thirty-one of the 32 planes were shot down; the only damage to our side was when one of the falling planes crashed on the cruiser *San Francisco*, Callaghan's flagship.

Toward evening the escorts saw our transports clear of the area and then returned. Word from the air reconnaissance was that half of the great Japanese armada had moved down to the Bougainville area and might attempt to run that night. It seemed an act of madness on the part of Callaghan to pit his little cruiser force against one that outnumbered him in that class alone and which could in addition bring to action the stout armor and heavy guns of battleships. His instructions were, in fact, to fight a delaying action; *Enterprise* was on the way from the south, again repaired. But this was the absolute crisis of the campaign, for if the enemy managed to put those troops ashore we might never be able to eject them from Guadalcanal. The American Admiral made his decision on that ground.

At a little after one o'clock the Japanese appeared on the radar screen—a column of cruisers and destroyers straight from the west of Savo Island, two battleships with more destroyers sweeping down from north of the same island, another cruiser and destroyer column at the leftward flank of the battleship, while somewhere behind was a group of transports. Callaghan swung sharply rightward to get across their bows, left again to close, and, just as the enemy searchlights snapped on, he opened fire.

The battle instantly became a melee at ranges so close that the leading enemy battleship could not depress her guns enough to hit our cruisers on the water line, so close that many of the torpedoes did not run far enough to actuate their firing mechanism. The American ships rushed generally between the lines of Japanese, though destroyers on both sides split off and turned in all directions. No one has succeeded in making a connected story of the events. Callaghan was killed and the whole upper half of his flagship wrecked by a salvo of 14-inch shells from a battleship; Admiral Norman Scott was killed and his flagship *Atlanta* so damaged that she sank the next day. Three of our destroyers went down and all the other vessels were more or less crippled. In revenge they had sent down two of the heavy Japanese flotilla leaders, almost cruisers for size and strength, and damaged several others. But the big dividend was the Japanese battleship *Hiyei*. She was discovered next morning near Savo Island, obviously in bad shape and trying to get away. The fliers poured out after her and hit her with enough torpedoes to sink her before night. Several of the torpedoes failed to explode—a common defect of that time.

WHAT was left of Callaghan's force of course had to withdraw from the area, and during the withdrawal we lost the anti-aircraft cruiser *Juneau*, torpedoed by a submarine which our destroyers were too much damaged to deal with. That night the Japanese came down the Slot again, with a force which subjected Henderson Field and our positions to the most intensive shelling they had yet received. There was apparently some flaw in the enemy arrangements at this point, for they made no attempt to deliver troops. Perhaps they expected the shelling would render the field inoperative and they could run their convoys in with impunity the following day.

They were wrong in two directions. The field was not wholly knocked out and the carrier *Enterprise* slipped up into the water south of Guadalcanal and flew off her planes in time to catch the convoy of twelve big transports (one an 18,000-ton liner) coming down the Slot in daylight. The first attack was on the escort. The *Enterprise* men sank a heavy cruiser and a destroyer and drove off the rest; then all the planes assailed the transports. Six went down with all hands, two were last seen afire and sinking. The remaining four beached on Guadalcanal during the early part of the night, but the men who got ashore from them were more ready for hospitalization than for battle.

But the transport movement was not the only element in the Japanese plan. They had moved their other battleship with a heavy cruiser squadron into position during the 14th and as night fell sent them down to cover the expected landing of their troops. *Enterprise's* operations south of the island had been covered by the battleships *Washington* and *South Dakota* under Rear-Admiral W. A. Lee. Our cruisers in the South Pacific were now all gone. Halsey, reluctant as he was to trust those heavy ships, the last he had, in the narrow reef-strewn waters of the Solomons by night where they could not avoid torpedoes, ordered them in. Lee and his two battleships with an escort of four destroyers circled Savo Island once and were bound west when the enemy appeared, flotilla leaders and destroyers coming around both sides of the island.

Both American battleships opened fire and each slaughtered one of the Japanese torpedo craft with her first salvo. The six to ten remaining Japanese light craft, led by a cruiser, rushed the battleships and in a brief, violent gun-torpedo action sank three of our destroyers and disabled the fourth, losing one or two of their units in the process. Before the bright gun flashes had died, the enemy battle line came charging down past the island, headed by a pair of cruisers that pinned *South Dakota* with their searchlights and riddled her upper works, but at the same moment she and *Washington* poured twelve rapid salvos without a miss into the leading Jap battleship, *Kirishima*. She turned on her side and sank through a whirlpool of flame in less than ten minutes. Their heavy cruisers were silenced, and what was left of the Japanese fleet turned in flight.

THE struggle for Guadalcanal, which had begun as a limited operation and ended by absorbing so much of the strength of both navies, was won. But the desperate three-day action which terminated the major fighting decided far more than whose flag should wave over the airfield on a remote

Pacific island. Materially it destroyed the Japanese South Pacific Fleet as an effective unit; spiritually, it completed the ruin of Japanese command morale begun at Coral Sea and Midway. The Japanese had thrown their ultimate reserves into the effort to recover the island and had not only lost but had had those reserves demolished in battle. Never again did a Japanese fleet willingly accept action against American warships. Their effort from this time forth was to distract, to wear down, to conduct operations by a process of attrition and dogged defense. The offensive spirit was gone; from now on they were playing for a draw. Previous to the Battle of Guadalcanal our own offensive had been on the basis of preventing the enemy from attacking elsewhere. We were now released from the compulsion of considering his moves.

CHAPTER V

THE virtual elimination of Port Darwin as a base by the Japanese air attack of February, 1942, left Port Moresby on the southern flank of the Papuan Peninsula as the only Allied outpost from which the Japanese imperial triangle could be approached by the way of Australia and the south. Throughout the summer of that year the enemy made persistent efforts toward eliminating it. The first failed when Wilson Brown's raid cut the supplies from the force which was to take the overland route. The second was broken up when the Japanese invasion force for the Louisiades turned back from the Battle of Coral Sea. But in mid-July the Japanese worked eastward along the coast from Lae and Salamaua to set up minor forward bases at Buna and Gona due north of Moresby beyond the Owen Stanley range. They began at once to work their specially trained jungle fighters up the pass. Late in the month they drove in the small Australian outpost at its crest and pushing on rapidly, placed Moresby under virtual siege by August 20.

At this moment they decided to clinch the matter. A convoy, organized along the usual Tokyo Express lines and operating by night along the shores to escape observation, threw a force of troops and laborers ashore at Milne Bay on the easternmost tip of New Guinea to set up a base and air strip there. It would give them a field on the south side of the mountains and would enable them to render all but impossible the shipment of heavy forces across Torres Strait, where they had already heavily hit one convoy in July by means of planes flying over the mountains.

But General MacArthur had not been idle in the meanwhile. The July convoy contained a full division of American troops and got most of them ashore, where they were able to hold the enemy in check outside Moresby. MacArthur had long since marked Milne Bay as a probable Japanese landing point, and as early as June he had moved in a strong force of Australian troops, keeping them well under concealment. The Japanese who landed were counterattacked before they could dig in, and were wiped out in a week of fighting. Fighters from the Port Moresby strip provided cover for an increasing number of bombers flown over from fields in Australia, and these bombers so persistently attacked supply dumps in the Buna-Gona region that the enemy facing Moresby was soon in grave difficulties both for food and ammunition. In September the Japanese began to retreat; Australian troops and a growing number of Americans pressed them back along the trails.

Like the Japanese during their advance, these troops found the beginning stages relatively easy, discovering more enemy dead of disease and malnutrition than of wounds, and receiving considerable help from the natives, who had been maltreated and antagonized by the Japanese. As the distance from Moresby increased, so did the supply difficulties that had stalled the Japanese campaign; everything used or eaten had to be carried on human backs. Through the latter part of September and most of October there was little movement. By that time the air officers on General MacArthur's staff had worked out a system of coöperation under which supplies could be dropped from planes. Japanese fighters that might have interfered were being drawn into the vortex of Guadalcanal and the first air-supplied troop movement in history began. On November 4, Kokodo at the head of the pass fell, and the Japanese, now evidently in grave straits, were driven rapidly down the northward slope.

By the date of the great sea fight off Guadalcanal both Gona and Buna were under siege by Allied troops—Australian at the former, American at the

The New Guinea Campaign

Prepared by Robert W. Galvin expressly for WAR FOR THE WORLD

latter. Three days later the Japanese attempted to run a Tokyo Express convoy of eight destroyers loaded with troops and supplies up to their massed bases. It was heavily hit both by Allied planes operating from Milne Bay and by a squadron of PT boats which had worked along the north shore from cove to cove, concealing themselves under the overhang of the jungle.

All the operations of this campaign were on an insignificant scale compared with the other theaters of war, even the land fighting on Guadalcanal. The jungle conditions would permit nothing else. But as it became increasingly clear that the movement of bodies of troops adequate to important operations could not be undertaken without air cover sufficient to protect transports, the Papuan campaign grew in importance. That jungle-covered peninsula controlled the only route by which the Japanese could obtain access to an area vital to the Allies without undertaking oceanic operations —that is, it was the only route along which they could readily recover their lost initiative. In addition, as long as our forces held Papua, the enemy could make no concentration at Rabaul—the necessary base for the Solomons—without detection and report by our aerial scouts.

AT the conference in Washington during December, 1941, among President Roosevelt, Prime Minister Churchill, and their leading military advisers, it had been decided that the war against the Axis powers in Europe should have preference, as they represented the more dangerous enemy. Throughout most of 1942, and despite intense pressure from Russia and her sympathizers for immediate action against the German-held Continent, this remained, however, a statement of purpose rather than a decision to perform. Space for a major base at Londonderry in Northern Ireland was granted to the United States, and American engineers began to set up installations there as rapidly as men and materials could be shipped. The first arrivals came in May, 1942, and there were soon several divisions on hand, which were processed through to England as rapidly as possible. The defects in training were clear after the large-scale raid on Dieppe, France, in August. Although largely conducted by much more experienced Canadian troops, the losses were very heavy and the gains insignificant.

Meanwhile an aircraft carrier (*Wasp*) and a fast battleship had joined the British home fleet as protection against any effort on the part of major German units, then based among the Norwegian fjords, to raid either transatlantic convoys or those bound for the White Sea coast of Russia, which was in great need of military supplies because so much of her industry had fallen into German hands during the invasion. Many of the ships in these Arctic convoys were American. The German surface craft never succeeded in reaching them, but attacks by submarines and torpedo planes from the Norwegian coast were so heavy and persistent that the losses were very great—those to the "July convoy" of 1942, for instance, reaching 80 percent of the participating cargo carriers.

Wasp greatly distinguished herself by making two high-speed runs into the Mediterranean (April and May) to fly off planes for Malta, then under an aerial siege that was to endure for another year. The May group of planes caught the unescorted German bombers in the air over the island and inflicted upon them losses heavier than any the

Germans had suffered since the Battle of Britain;
it was a not inconsiderable factor in upsetting the
Nazi schedule and saving the island. But throughout this period most of the American naval activity
was on the home side of the Atlantic.

This was partly due to the presence at Marti-
nique in the West Indies of a big French aircraft
carrier and a cruiser under an officer of known loy-
alty to the German-dominated Vichy Government.
The place had to be kept under a watch that
amounted to blockade. But this was only a minor
factor. Almost as soon as Germany declared war
she directed major portions of her submarine fleet
against the American East-coast ports. The first
sinking occurred on January 14, 1942; after that
sinkings followed rapidly, the submarines remaining
under water on the ledge of the continental shelf
during the day and rising at night to catch ships
silhouetted against the lights of cities along the
shore. Vessels were sunk within sight of people
standing on the New Jersey coast. There was soon
a serious oil shortage as a result of losses among
the tankers which normally brought a great part
of the East-coast supply from Texas and, twice, the
entire entrance to the Chesapeake Bay area was
under genuine blockade, with all sailings inter-
dicted, principally because of the activity of minelaying submarines.

The navy hesitated to use the convoy system

because it would aggravate the over-all shortage
of bottoms by delaying many vessels till convoys
could be made up, and by restraining all to the
speed of the slowest ship in convoy—also because
adequate escorts were lacking. The Pacific ab-
sorbed an enormous number of destroyers for fleet
duties; many more were needed to protect the
long-range oversea convoys to England and Russia.
Of light antisubmarine craft there were practically
none at the outbreak of the war. Aerial operations
against U-boats were hampered by the Navy's
need for its own long-range patrol-type flying boats
in the Pacific and by the fact that army pilots
operating from bases along the shore were completely lacking in experience, especially in identi-
fication. (One army pilot reported Ambrose light-
ship off New York harbor as a submarine and another attempted to bomb an American destroyer
near Newport.)

The problem was thus quadruple—passive defense, production, organization, and training, the
latter with particular reference to such devices as
radar and sonic detectors, which are extremely
efficient in the hands of experienced personnel but
well-nigh useless in those of amateurs. Comparatively speaking, the training problem was the easi-
est to solve. Army aviators operating from bases
close along the coast were able to make their
flights at once operational and instructional, and

while no very sensational results were obtained down to November, 1942 (there is not a single indubitable instance of a U-boat sunk by an army plane during this period), they exercised a restricting influence on the raiders.

The process was aided by the establishment of the Sea Frontier system in May, under which army and navy units operated under a single command in coastal work, officers of the two services occupying desks side by side and pooling resources as well as information. Under this joint command a "brownout" of the city lights that had been so useful to the submarines was imposed by the army, and a system of gasoline and oil rationing was set up to relieve the tanker shortage. The greatest help, however, came from the production gains. The navy already had a program for the expansion of its service of blimps—small nonrigid dirigibles—when the war began. Along the coast in an area where they were not subject to enemy air attacks these craft proved extraordinarily successful as antisubmarine scouts, because of their ability to hover in flight. It was claimed that no ship under blimp convoy was sunk.

But to draw maximum results from the blimps and the increasing number of planes, the support of surface vessels was necessary, not only in their capacity as counterattackers but also to keep the submarines so far below the surface that they could

not conduct efficient operations. At the beginning
of the war there were available only some old destroyers from the last war, together with a number
of Coast Guard cutters and pleasure boats converted to the same purpose. The latter could carry
a couple of depth charges but no artillery that
would disturb a submarine; in May a U-boat sur-
faced off the Virginia Capes and sank two of these
improvised cutters by gunfire.

But that month the production of antisubmarine
vessels began to attain respectable figures. There
were already in existence the designs for the excellent 110-foot wooden submarine chasers that
had done so much service in the last war. Massive
production orders were placed immediately for
these with small boat firms all along the coast,
while large numbers of a new type, 173 feet long
and with a steel hull, were also laid down. An antisubmarine training command was established at
Miami near the bottleneck point where U-boats
liked to lie in wait for tankers coming up from the
Gulf of Mexico. By May, the key date in many
features of the antisubmarine war, both types of
chaser were on duty along the Atlantic coast in
such numbers as to make the station precarious
for the Germans. Some ten or eleven submarines
were sunk and the destruction of shipping fell off
sharply.

An additional reason for this apparent gain was

that the Nazis had transferred the bulk of their activities to the Caribbean, where the wartime demand for oil had temporarily raised the refinery harbor of Curaçao to the position of the third port in the world. The situation there immediately became far more critical than it had been farther north, since the means of defense were almost completely lacking, and even when the submarine chasers began to appear the wooden type proved to have insufficient fuel capacity for operations over the distance involved. During the summer the depredations of the raiders were so extensive that one third of all the tonnage sunk by submarines went down in the Caribbean; and among the smaller islands which depend upon imports for a large proportion of their food there was actual hunger. Ships were sunk in plain sight of Trinidad and Guantanamo, the convoy control points, and one submarine shelled the refineries at Aruba.

By October the larger submarine chasers were arriving in quantities sufficient to provide convoys with effective escort, and the counteroffensive had gained enormously by the appearance of squadrons of new patrol planes equipped with radar, which permitted them to operate at night when the U-boats came to the surface to recharge their batteries and to communicate with home bases. October saw Caribbean shipping, particularly the hard-pressed tankers, taking as heavy losses as in any month of the war, but the submarines also took their heaviest loss—losses so severe that even had the African expedition not brought an entirely new factor into the strategic situation, it is probable that the Nazis would still have relaxed their efforts off the American coast.

When defenses became strong the submarines were always quick to shift the incidence of their attack. How effective it had been was revealed when Admiral W. D. Leahy, Chief of Staff to President Roosevelt, could make no better announcement at the end of eleven months of war than that the Allies "had almost as much shipping available" as at the beginning of the conflict. During that interval, 6,800,000 gross tons had been constructed; over 8,000,000 had been sunk.

ONE of the first steps undertaken after the declaration of war in December, 1941, was the reorganization of the army from the lateral basis under which infantry, cavalry, field and heavy artillery remained separate entities till the troops actually passed into the control of the field commanders, to a vertical basis, with three services—ground forces, service forces, and air forces—meeting only under General George C. Marshall, nominally the Chief of Staff of the Army, but in practice its commander.

The Combined Chiefs of Staff early decided to

enter upon a program of long-range bombardments of Germany and when they could be reached, the installations of the Japanese. The physical instruments of the program were the B-24 (Liberator) and B-17 (Flying Fortress) four-engined bombers, much resembling each other in being high-speed planes with powerful defensive armament, intended to operate over enemy territory in broad daylight at upper altitudes and obtain results by the precision with which they placed bombs on the target through the use of the Norden bombsight. This precision was only relative, of course; later surveys showed misses by as much as two miles (though not exactly common); in general, high-level bombing can never be described as accurate. But it seemed better than the area bombing. The theory was vigorously contested by the British, who had tried out early models of the Flying Fortress without the defensive powers of those that followed and had seen several of them shot down without achieving anything like commensurate damage. Their own heavy bombers operated at night, carrying nearly twice the load of a B-17, and their method was to distribute explosives over an industrial area without attempting to hit specific targets.

The bombing program was very slow in getting under way, the first B-17 arriving in England (by flight across the Atlantic) only on July 4, 1942. That same day a group of six American pilots conducted the first bombing of German-held territory in Holland with light bombers borrowed from the British. They displayed much courage but achieved small success, losing two of their planes and having a third wrecked, while two of the remainder brought back their loads of bombs. But by August 17, Brigadier-General Ira Eaker, commanding the Eighth Air Force (this was the designation of the England-based command) was able to stage an experimental raid on the railroad yards at Rouen with twelve machines. The bombing results were judged good, but the planes had such heavy fighter cover from the RAF, and diversionary tactics were so successful, that there was no opposition to speak of.

The first real test came on August 21, when nine B-17s that had missed their rendezvous with fighter cover were attacked over Holland by 25 German fighters and beat them off without loss while two of the Nazis were shot down. It was only a small-scale action and the British leaders who wanted our bombers to fly with them on the night area attacks remained skeptical. But after several other minor raids whose purpose was fundamentally that of training the crews, General Eaker felt confident enough to send 100 of his big bombers to Lille on October 9, in the first major daylight attack. The place was important to the Germans both industrially and as a rail center. It was elaborately defended by fighters from all over North France; a furious air battle resulted. Four of the big bombers were shot down; but in return they destroyed 21 German fighters certainly, with as many more probably, and the raid was not prevented.

With this dramatic victory, reversing all the precedents of aerial war in respect to the vulnerability of bombers, major aerial operations closed down for the winter. Two air groups—well over 200 planes—were withdrawn from General Eaker's command to form the nucleus of the new 12th Air Force for the support of the African invasion, as the storms and overcast of a European winter were not suitable for the American type of operation in the north.

To command the American forces in Europe General Marshall had chose General Dwight D. Eisenhower, a comparatively unknown officer who had been occupied chiefly with staff employments. In order to prevent potential enemies from working up a file on his methods and thought patterns, as the Germans were fond of doing, Eisenhower had been somewhat deliberately kept in the background after his selection for high command. His outstanding characteristics were two: he possessed a remarkable ability to persuade people of widely divergent views and training to work together, and an equally unusual capacity for perceiving how to accomplish something not expected by the enemy because of its "impossibility."

It is not easy to assign with accuracy the part played by any individual in making the strategic plan for a war whose major decisions were so almost entirely reached in committee. But if the decision to deliver the first attack on Hitler's "Fortress Europe" by way of French Africa bears something of the impress of Roosevelt's mind (who throughout the struggle was at the utmost pains to take steps that might rally possible allies) and Churchill's (who stood throughout for an attack on "the soft underbelly" of Europe), it also bears that of Eisenhower and his doctrine of the unexpected. Clearly enough, something had to be attempted to draw the Germans from the death grip they had obtained on Russia by driving to the Volga and laying siege to the industrial city of Stalingrad. If that place fell, the Nazis would cut the main Red armies off from their only important source of fuel; and, as the summer wore away with the Germans making persistent gains and the Russians taking frightful losses, it seemed to the despairing Allied nations of the West that Stalingrad must fall.

Early in October a submarine had carried Eisenhower's must trusted staff officer, Colonel Mark Clark, to Algiers where, at a secret midnight conference, arrangements were reached with Admiral Darlan and other key figures among the group who governed Africa in the name of the German-dominated Vichy Government of France. Both the Germans and Vichy itself were not altogether ignorant that something was going on, but they seemed to have suspected an attack on Dakar, far to the south. Dakar was of primary importance because much of the French naval strength was concentrated there and because of its proximity to the route around Africa by which many of the supplies for hard-pressed Russia were reaching the Persian Gulf and all those for the British Army striving to hold the borders of Europe were reaching the Red Sea.

The decision was nevertheless to move into North Africa. Two big convoys from England carrying troops partly American but primarily British entered the Mediterranean. A far larger, all-American force sailed directly from the United States for Morocco and that part of Africa that looks on the Atlantic. Before dawn on November 8, landing forces moved in at four points—Oran and Algiers in Algeria, Casablanca and Port Lyautey in Morocco. At Algiers everything had been arranged; the American troops who were first ashore east and west of the city were met by guides and by the afternoon of that day were in possession of the town as well as the person of Admiral Darlan, the Deputy Chief of State of the Vichy Government. British formations filed in behind and presently also began to land at Bougie, up near the Tunisian border under British General K. A. N. Anderson. Attempts to penetrate deeper, to Bizerte, would have deprived the operation of all surprise (it could easily have been seen by scouting aircraft) and would have exposed the expedition to the attack of powerful Italian surface units.

At Oran there was stiff resistance: several British ships were lost in breaking through the boom in the harbor, and the Ranger battalions that attempted the first landing on the waterfront were badly cut up without effecting anything. British ships and planes from Gibraltar provided fire cover, and by afternoon fairly strong forces were ashore. The French held hard in fortified positions and their artillery fire was very accurate, but they had neither planes nor any power of movement, and throughout the two following days were gradually pushed back into pockets of resistance by strong British forces.

The heaviest fighting was at Casablanca, the site of the main effort. No deal had been made with the Vichy leadership there, apart from some understandings with members of the underground. The harbor held a light cruiser, two submarines, six giant destroyers and an unfinished battleship that was nevertheless fully able to use her guns. As the American fleet approached, the French battleship opened fire and the lighter ships dashed out to attack our covering forces, which were about evenly divided between very new ships fresh from the yards and very old ships reconditioned for this expedition. Only a miracle could have given the French forces any success against the overwhelming firepower brought to bear. There was no miracle. All the light French craft were quickly sunk, and though the battleship continued to fire for some time, she was silenced and sunk where she lay by the coöperation of our dive bombers and the guns of the new battleship *Massachusetts*, firing by radar control from a distance of nearly 20 miles.

The landing parties made good their beachheads on both sides of the town under fire that was accurate enough to cause some casualties; and with considerable fumbling, for these troops were as yet amateurs, they began to work into the back country. Off shore a group of German submarines that had been trailing the convoy got in among the lined-up ships and sank three transports. But the campaign never had a chance to develop; on the 11th of November the Germans moved in to occupy all France and the following morning Admiral Darlan ordered French units in Africa to cease fire and to coöperate with the Allies.

One week earlier Marshal Montgomery of the British army had launched an offensive at El

Alamein on the frontiers of Egypt and by a brilliant victory had sent the Afrika Korps of German Marshal Rommel rolling back in disorderly rout from that high-water mark of Hitler's fortunes. Four days later a Japanese battleship went down before the eyes of Admiral Lee off Guadalcanal; a week later the Russians seized the offensive against the Germans battling in the Caucasus and the ruins of Stalingrad. In that fortnight of November a world decision had been reached; the Axis could not carry its initial offensive thrust through to victory, and the period of defense and preparation for the American forces was ended.

CHAPTER VI

THE CAMPAIGN IN TUNISIA

THERE were no Axis forces in Tunisia except the usual agents when the Allies landed farther west on November 8, 1942. But the enemy reaction was prompt and vigorous, as it was of great moral importance to turn this first offensive effort of the Western Allies into a failure, and of considerable military importance to prevent their gaining a *point d'appui* from which Italy, the weak partner in the Axis, could be attacked direct.

Estimates by competent military men were that to make a direct attack would require nearly all the British fleet and half the American with the full air forces of both nations; nevertheless there was a considerable body of opinion that the enterprise should be undertaken.

Transport planes in considerable number were used to carry German troops into Tunisia, a large portion of the dwindling Italian merchant marine brought more, and when the British raided these convoys with light craft and submarines, there put in an appearance a new type of troop carrier on the run from Sicily—the Siebel Ferry, motor-driven and stoutly enough armored to resist the attacks of strafing planes, but with so shallow a draft that torpedoes would pass right under the craft. In the early stages at least a thousand men a day were landed by such methods, and this was far faster than we could bring men to the same area, either by water or by the overland route. The command was given to General Bernd von Arnim.

General Eisenhower had taken over the direction of the African front when the invasion was launched, leaving General Jacob L. Devers as com-mander of our troops in England. It seemed to General Eisenhower that when the French capitu-lated so rapidly and joined their forces to ours (American casualties were less than 2,000) a quick push might win all Tunisia. This would have the enormous strategic advantage of cutting off the German Afrika Korps, now making its way back across the deserts of Libya. The order was accord-ingly given, General Alexander receiving command at the front, since the majority of the forces in-volved belonged to his nation. The country is one of few and poor roads between steep, table-shaped mountains, a fact which determined the direction and emphasis of military movement.

A British column was thrust westward from Bougie and Bone along the coast road toward the

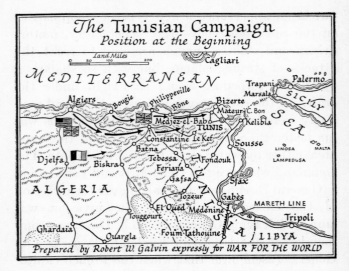

The Tunisian Campaign
Position at the Beginning

Prepared by Robert W. Galvin expressly for WAR FOR THE WORLD

great fortress and naval base at Bizerte. A second, heavier, column moved out of Algiers along the main highway, which swings south (to get through the Grand Dorsal range that covers the western border of Tunisia), and then north again to reach Tunis city. The second column included the American troops of the Algiers expedition, but none above a reinforced battalion in strength. Out on the right of the same column the French troops from Algeria covered the flank and moved toward the secondary port of Sousse. Parachutists were freely used, especially in efforts to gain advanced airfields for Allied planes.

The first clashes came on November 18–19, just

west of the Tunisian border in the case of the coastal column, and outside the important road center of Medjez-El-Bab in the case of the column operating from Algiers against Tunis. On the north the British drove in a German counterattack, which retreated behind a screen of demolitions and land mines. On the south there was heavy fighting but the British could make no gain, and when the French column intervened it got badly mauled, being poorly equipped and without air support while the Nazis brought numerous bombers into play. This determined General Alexander to make an attack in form with a mixed column of French-British-American troops along a line from Mateur to Medjez-El-Bab.

The date was November 24, and the attackers had the help of some American bombers which had staged in from Morocco to use the single very inefficient airfield now available. The attack took Medjez-El-Bab, and the central mixed detachment worked all the way through Tebourba to Djedlida and destroyed 40 German planes on the airfield there. But the Mateur column had no success, and most of the central mixed detachment was shifted north to support it. The Germans promptly retook Djedeida and a number of prisoners in a vigorous counterattack.

Two days later the Germans violently counterattacked Tebourba, just as General Alexander was preparing another move at the ends of his line. The Allied Tebourba detachment was broken up or thrown off, and troops of the American 1st Division arrived only in time to prevent a major gap being opened at the center of the Allied line. When the Germans again attacked on December 3, the entire Allied front had to be withdrawn to a line running north and south from 15 miles west of Mateur (in German hands) to Medjez-El-Bab (in ours) and then southward.

The advance was clearly stalled by the fact that the German line of reinforcement was the shorter and more convenient. Operations settled down to a war of minor attacks and position improvements for both sides, in one of which on Christmas Eve some green American formations took a beating and lost a couple of crests. With the front closing down for the winter, the section north of Medjez-El-Bab was held by British, the center by American, and the extreme south by French troops.

There was a good deal of talk on the Allied side about bad roads and heavy rains, which prevented the movement of transport, and of the necessity of keeping forces in northern Morocco to watch the equivocal conduct of fascist Spain across the border. But the basic fact was that the Germans could and did reach Tunisia more rapidly by the short route from Sicily than the Allies could by the long one from Casablanca. We had only a single line of railroad which, even when bolstered by American-made rolling stock, remained inadequate and in bad condition. Algiers, Bougie, and Bone were used to some extent, but they were so continually under attack from Axis bombers based in Sicily that the shipping losses were very heavy at a time when shipping losses could not be afforded. Nor could Allied air strength be readily built up to drive the enemy bombers off, because of the lack of cover at prospective fields and the immense demands air power would make on the already overworked transportation system for shop equipment, gasoline, and the heavy steel mats for landing strips.

In this first exchange, each side had learned about the other much that was to remain fairly constant throughout the war. The Americans had found that the German soldier was an exceptionally skilled infantry fighter, especially in scouting and patroling; tenacious in position; successful in his use of land mines, of which his government had supplied enormous quantities. He was possessed of a superior artillery piece in the 88 millimeter, which was used against aircraft, tanks, and personnel.

In return the Germans had received a distinctly unpleasant shock in the firing speed and accuracy of American light artillery, more formidable than any they had encountered, even in Russia. Our fighter pilots were on the whole better than theirs, fast becoming more numerous, and when the P-38 Lightnings arrived, were flying the better planes, so that German air attacks had to be made by stealth and were heavily paid for. Worst of all for the Germans, the tank columns that had run unchecked from Marseille to Moscow no longer succeeded.

This was principally the result of a technical invention, the bazooka, handled by two men and firing a rocket shell which would crush in the wall of a concrete pillbox or of any tank the Nazis then had. A few had been used by Marshal Montgomery's forces in his attack in Egypt; in Tunisia they appeared in quantity and stalled every attempt on the part of General von Arnim to turn his local counterattack victories into a general offensive. Von Arnim had also discovered that although he could move troops in Tunisia more readily than the Allies, it was far less easy to keep them supplied under the growing weight of Allied air power and the British navy—a fact which contributed no little to the German decision not to make Tunisia a major theater of war.

DURING January, 1943, the Axis heavily attacked the French troops at the extreme south of the line around Point du Fahs and drove them back seven miles under considerable losses to make room for the entry into Tunisia of Marshal Rommel and his

Afrika Korps, who had been retreating deliberately along the Tripolitan shore, holding up Montgomery's pursuit by demolitions, extensive minefields, and by the abandonment of their Italian allies. At the end of January, Rommel was within the Mareth Line—an elaborate system of prepared concrete fortifications facing eastward, now without guns or stores but still formidable. North and west of this, a chain of salt lakes, swamps, and depressions runs 250 miles back to meet the great desert, leaving only a narrow neck of passable ground at Gabès. In the Mareth Line Rommel left three Italian divisions as a rear guard; with his own troops he plugged the Gabès gap and on February 14 threw all the armored forces he could gather into a great attack on the American positions at Faid Pass, where we had most deeply penetrated Tunisia.

In the center of this attack were a number of Mark VI tanks, so heavily armored as to be practically immune to bazooka fire, but the essential features of the attack were that it had local command of the air, that it was concentrated, and that our troops were surprised. It gained 18 miles the first day and cut off many of the formations along our front. Next day an American armored force counterattacked and recovered part of this, but the Germans had worked strong armored formations through the hills behind our right flank, and on the 16th they attacked simultaneously from front and rear with strong air support. Our tanks were badly outnumbered and individually no match for the heavy Mark VIs. In a running fight the American armor was practically destroyed and the encircled formations had to be abandoned.

The Germans pushed right on across a wide valley to the next line of hills, where the little town of Kasserine covers the pass of the same name and the road to the main American base at Tebessa. On February 20 the Germans attacked this gap by working infantry up the draws in the flanking mountains, then rushed through the gap itself a strong armored column which once more got in the rear of American infantry forces and caused them heavy loss. Nothing but darkness and distance held the enemy this day, and on the morning of the 21st Rommel attacked again in two columns, one toward Tebessa and the other toward Thala on its northeastward plain.

But Thala was now held by strong formations of experienced British infantry which had been rushed from the north by forced marches. Both at that point and at Tebessa, American artillery was in position, sent forward to the exclusion of everything else. Moreover, American aviation had been concentrated and had wrenched from the enemy his command of the skies. The Thala attack broke down before noon with the Germans losing heavily in tanks. In the afternoon that of

Tebessa also failed, and during the night Rommel retreated, abandoning the whole valley back to the high hills around Faid Pass which gave him artillery observation posts.

The operation exerted a depressing effect on American morale and correspondingly elevated that of the Germans, who had inflicted on us casualties equal to the full strength of an infanry division and who had captured more equipment in tanks, guns, and trucks than they lost. Several officers, including Major General L. W. Friedendall, commanding the II Corps on which the blow had fallen, were sent home. In truth the American tactical performance had been very bad, the scouting poorly performed, units widely parceled out and fed into action in small groups to be cut to pieces in detail.

The strategic result was that the Germans had been able to possess themselves of a double mountain barrier along their westward flank at the southern end of their Tunisian bastion. A full campaign with attendant delay and casualties would be necessary before they were dislodged. But if they had won the small game, they had failed to gain the big one: their effort to capture the American base and to win through to the rear of the British in the north, where the heaviest forces were in play, had failed. General Eisenhower's plans were delayed, altered in detail, but not dis-

rupted. An attack against British positions in the
north to prevent their sending aid to the hard-
pressed Americans at Kasserine had broken down
with considerable casualties.

WITH the slackening of the Tunisian rains in middle March, 1943, and the installation of new airfields, the Allies were ready for an advance. They
had in line the British First Army holding from
the Mediterranean to just north of Medjez-El-Bab;
the French XIX Corps, the old Algerian army now
well supplied with American equipment except in
tanks, from Medjez-El-Bab to near Faid Pass; the
United States II Corps (now under Major General
George S. Patton, an armored forces specialist)
from Faid to Gafsa; and a French desert corps that
had come all across Africa to furnish the link with
Montgomery's forces before the Mareth Line.

The Axis allies, much outnumbered, had about
150,000 men in the north and about 100,000 of Rommel's old Afrika Korps south of the Gabès bottleneck and in the Mareth Line, whose positions they
mostly neglected for a new series of strongpoints
constructed by their own engineers. Everywhere
they had dug themselves well in behind extensive
minefields during the winter, building concreted
positions that had interlocking fields of fire and
were skillfully camouflaged. Everywhere they had
forward observation posts on peaks, with artillery

on reverse slopes behind which it could not be reached.

The Eisenhower-Alexander plan was to destroy the force south of Gabès. Montgomery was to send a mobile wing round the flank of the line between it and the region of salt marsh, at the same time attacking with other forces on the front to pin the Germans down. The American II Corps was to attack straight across the ridges behind Gabès, while the French XIX covered their flank by a move northeast up the valleys.

The attack opened on the night of March 20 on the Mareth front. It rained in torrents that night, turning the wadi before the German position into a bog which the British were unable to penetrate—they suffered considerable casualties as they tried to build a causeway for the passage of armor. The turning column marched slowly in an effort to keep its movements secret and did not attack till the 22nd, by which time the Germans had divined its purpose. An armored division held this advance to minor gains for two days, at which time Montgomery swung his whole armored strength to this flank while the French desert corps attacked the massif of Mt. Tebega, which barred the path.

There was a good deal of hard fighting here as well as in a renewal of the attack on the Mareth positions, but no wide gains were scored. However, the German commander lost heavily and found himself so weakened that he decided to pull out, covering his retreat with extensive minefields and strong rear guards. Another stand was made along the line Mt. Tebega-Wadi El Akarit, but Montgomery flanked this too by the left in an attack beginning April 4, and the Germans went back a full 150 miles through the Gabès gap to where the high rough-tangled mountains that form the keel of Cape Bon Peninsula extend inland to make a position that can be held by relatively few men.

During all this campaign the American II Corps had been trying to penetrate through Maknassy and Kairouan onto the German rear. The move came to nothing, every attack stalling amid the minefields and under counterattacks of about a battalion strength, with which the Germans very skillfully broke the point of each American advance. Farther north the British First Army hewed away at the enemy defenses and made gains territorially small, but including the bulk of the positions so carefully fortified during the winter.

The campaign ended on April 13 without obtaining its objective of destroying the Axis southern force. But the enemy had been severely hurt. His casualties were much larger than ours, thanks chiefly to the efficiency of the American air force, which could now obtain full command of the air whenever desired and which harried German movements unremittingly, again and again hounding them out of their best artillery positions. Moreover, our planes with the cooperation of the British sea forces had now made it almost impossible for the Germans to obtain either reinforcements or supplies, while the transportation difficulties in our rear were now mostly solved, and fresh bodies of American troops were reaching the front in a flood. Finally, Montgomery's Eighth Army was linked with the other Allied forces and all were under a single command.

FOR the next assault Generals Eisenhower and Alexander reshuffled their forces. The French were given the sector in the extreme north, next to the sea. From this point down to Medjez-El-Bab the American II Corps, now four divisions strong, took over under General Omar Bradley, former head of the Infantry School, an officer who, like Eisenhower, had been rather deliberately held in the background after his extreme skill in tactics had caused General Marshall to mark him for future high command. From Medjez-El-Bab to Point du Fahs and including one end of the broad Medjerda Valley, the British First Army was stationed and to it were added three of the best divisions from their Eighth Army, brought round secretly behind the front. They left their artillery behind them with the remainder of the Eighth,

The Tunisian Campaign
Closing Operations

LEGEND
— Main Roads
＋＋＋＋ Railroads
1240 Elevations in Feet

N

Land Miles
0   5   10   20

Cape Serrat

Cape Blanc
Bechater
BIZERTE
Metline
El Azib
Lake Bizerta
Ferryville
Porto Farina
Mateur
1292
Gulf
of
Tunis
Protville
Medjerda
HILL 609
Chouigui
La Marsa
Sidi Nsir
Sidi bou Saïd
Djedeida
Beja
St. Cyprien
TUNIS
LONG STOP HILL
Medjez-el-Bab
Sidi Medien 1193
1443
Goubellat
Ain el Asker
Grombalia
Miliane
Smindja
Bou Arada
2224
Zaghouan
4250
Pont du Fahs
DAM
Djebibina
Takrouna
Enfidaville

Prepared by Robert W. Galvin expressly for WAR FOR THE WORLD

which held the front from around Enfidaville to a region of desert and butte, where a small French formation was shoved in between the two British armies. The total Allied forces outnumbered their opponents in the proportion of seven to five, which is no great superiority on the ground.

The failure to move the Eighth Army's artillery was deliberate. On the night of April 19, 1943, it opened a prodigious fire near Enfidaville and at dawn the Eighth attacked, with the design of convincing Von Arnim that this force, which had carried much of the load of the African fighting, was to make the main assault. Actually that assault was to be made at the center, one British column working straight through Medjez-El-Bab along the main highway toward Tunis while another moved up the Medjerda Valley on the same point to cut the Axis-held territory in two, while the American troops attacked in conformity toward Bizerte.

The German general was completely deceived and moved the bulk of his reserves to the south with armor in the rear for a counterattack. As a result, the American II Corps made slow but steady progress with comparatively light casualties along the road through Mateur, but the British advance in Medjerda Valley was stalled in a violent tank battle on April 27 and that through Medjez-El-Bab ran into a steep, bald hill, Djebel Bou Aoukaz. Through its artillery observation posts the hill dominated the whole region; twice, the British were driven from it after having gained lodgments. Further efforts around Point du Fahs failing, the British First regrouped for a push against this mountain with all troops in, while the air forces received a mission of sealing off the sector by breaking all communications.

Meanwhile, because the II Corps had hit him so hard, General Von Arnim had decided to abandon Bizerte (the place had been bombed into uselessness as a port) and to conduct his main defense along the hills running from Medjez-El-Bab northeast to the sea. His trucks of supplies preceding the troops began to move on May 2 or 3. At dawn on May 6 the British hit Djebel Bou Aoukaz and its region with nine divisions, two of them armored. An immense concentration of planes drove every German machine from the skies; support elements moved up to the attack in tight columns and so completely destroyed enemy communication points that headquarters in Tunis was unaware of what was passing at the front. By evening of the 6th the mountain was taken and the British were fanning out behind; by afternoon of the 7th they were in Tunis city, capturing many German officers in cafés.

That same day an American advance guard penetrated the great base city of Bizerte against weak opposition and pushed on after some 30,000

Axis troops isolated by the capture of Tunis, all of whom surrendered on May 9. The British armor that reached Tunis swung south against a weak line improvised by the enemy along the Miliane River and on the 11th captured 25,000 more Axis soldiers near Point du Fahs. A new attack by the Eighth Army having broken through, all the rest of the Axis troops in Tunisia surrendered by the 13th.

It had been primarily a British victory, to which the main American contributions were supplies, General Eisenhower's strategic sense and his ability to get coöperation from subordinates with widely different training and points of view, and the work of the Army Air Force. The latter, indeed, exceeded expectations. Its fighters dominated the front and on one occasion shot down an entire convoy of 23 giant six-motored transports in which the Germans were attempting to evacuate specialists and command personnel before the final debacle. Our heavy bombers made Axis shipping unsafe, especially in home harbors, and prevented the enemy from sending convoys by attacking their escorts, sinking one cruiser at Palermo and another as far away as the coast of Sardinia. Perhaps even more important, the light bombers gave close support to every movement, and in the final campaign acted brilliantly as forward artillery against those German positions on the reverse slopes which had previously proved so troublesome. The American ground troops, except for the artillery, still apparently had a good deal to learn. Their casualties had been under 20,-000, which demonstrates how comparatively little they had been engaged.

CHAPTER VII

THE ITALIAN BATTLEGROUND

WHEN a conference was held at Casablanca in
January, 1943, including not only Roosevelt and
Churchill but also their chief military advisers, it
was considered certain that, as far as the Axis was
concerned, the growing Allied air and naval power
in the Mediterranean would turn Africa into an un-
supportable island position by early summer. This
led to a decision to invade the great island of Sicily
on the date of the first favorable moon in July.
When the Tunisian bastion fell the plans were
pushed on apace. The first step was the siege of the
small Italian fortress-island of Pantelleria in the
straits. The siege began on May 22 with relays of
bombers from all over North Africa attacking the
place continually, while swarms of Allied fighters
kept any Axis aircraft from interfering.

The Italian anti-aircraft positions were put out
of commission early in the siege and the bombers
had no interruption till June 11, when the island
surrendered, less because of casualties than because
the water supply had run short and the morale of

the defenders had collapsed under the strain. The island's air strip was immediately reconditioned for use by Allied fighters which, with bombers from North Africa and further fighters from Malta, provided the air cover for the whole operation.

This was under the immediate command of General Alexander, but like the rearrangement that led to the Tunisian victory, bears the impress of Eisenhower's technique of the unexpected attack. Sicily offers comparatively long stretches of beach on which landings may be made, mainly from Gela on the southern shore northwestward to the region of Marsala, with another group on the eastern shore from Syracuse north to the slopes of Mt. Etna. These beaches the Axis had defended with an elaborate system of mines and underwater obstacles. There are numerous small towns both at the water's edge and close behind it, built of enduring stone. They were converted into fortresses with artillery positions and tank traps. In these various positions were three divisions of Italian coastal troops. Behind them, in concentration areas well hidden from Allied aircraft and beyond the range of guns afloat, were three German and two Italian infantry divisions, and two German armored divisions.

The Allies chose for attack the extreme southeastern angle of the island, where the beaches were by no means as good but the defenses distinctly second rate. The operation was conducted by two armies, the British Eighth (not the unit of the same name that had fought across Africa, many of its troops having been withdrawn for the invasion of France, already in view) and the new United States Seventh, under command of General Patton. The latter included the old II Corps (like the British Eighth, with many changes) and a provisional corps under Major-General Lucian K. Truscott, a division and a half strong. At dawn of July 11th the British, operating from Malta and the Tunisian ports, hit the beaches from Cape Pessaro northward to near Syracuse, with a groupment of Canadians on their left flank to link up with the American forces which struck at all the available points east of Licata. Both the British and Americans used strong forces of parachutists to leapfrog ahead of the advancing armies and seize airfields in the interior; both made extensive use of new types of shallow-draft landing craft operating between ship and shore, and of new types of amphibious supply vehicles.

It was in fact a shooting rehearsal for the major invasion of Europe that would have to take place some day, and as such it was fortunate that the forces engaged were limited and that General Eisenhower's strategy brought the initial blow against the unstable Italian coastal divisions just where they were weakest. A storm and heavy sea came up during the night to make the landings of both British and Canadians extremely difficult. The same gale dispersed the planes carrying the American parachutists, who landed anywhere from 30 to 50 miles from their intended positions; their influence was mainly upon the enemy's state of mind through attacks on his communications.

The first group of British parachutists were also off course but managed to reach the ground somewhere near the assigned positions and took the airfield desired. However, they came in a series of waves; before the second wave could arrive the Germans reassembled and won the field back. These events left the Axis forces with more air support than had been bargained on, and when it was clear that the Americans were encountering difficulties in getting heavy equipment through the surf at Gela, the Axis commander was encouraged to launch a powerful armored counterattack supported by Italian infantry against our II Corps. This was designed to cut the landing force in half; a covering attack was organized in the direction of Syracuse.

The Gela attack fell just after 8 A.M., when our 1st Division held a beachhead about seven miles long and two and a half deep with comparatively little artillery and only three tanks as yet ashore. It was a triple drive from three sides. The north wing had good cover and made some progress; that from the east a great deal, coming right down the beach to Division Headquarters. The situation was saved by the intervention of a light cruiser and a pair of destroyers which knocked out tank after tank from offshore and prevented the formation of any heavy enemy troop concentrations. The attack was rolled back with loss. That against the British never got under way, as the British had obtained possession of a mountain pass east of Syracuse. They captured that city with ease.

The American 1st Division now turned west, taking Licata the next day, while the 45th swung eastward and after a day of hard fighting captured an airfield at Biscati. That night it was planned to bring in most of the 82nd Airborne Division close behind our front lines in anticipation of a new Axis counterattack. The transport planes were blown slightly off course. At the same time German night bombers made a foray against the beachhead, with the result that our own anti-aircraft opened up maximum fire, shooting down 23 of our transports and completely riddling the 82nd Division; the men who did reach ground found themselves in the midst of a German artillery concentration.

The news was suppressed for a long time and caused considerable indignation at home when it did come out, but the strategic effect was small. By July 15 the Axis command estimated we had over ten divisions ashore, with air support that

The Invasion of Sicily

Prepared by Robert W. Galvin expressly for WAR FOR THE WORLD~

limited their own operations to reconnaissance and
night raids. They decided it was useless to hold
in open country against such forces, and moved to
concentrate their defenses in the northeastern portion of the island. Mt. Etna was the anchor of the
new line, and the fortified city of Catania, protected by a river in front, stood as an outwork.
From Etna a range of mountains runs westward
close along the northern shore, throwing to the sea
a series of steep ridges across which the coast road
runs. These ridges were to be held successively.

General Patton's forces, pushing both west along
the coast and northwest toward Palermo, accordingly encountered decreasing resistance. Palermo

fell on July 22 and the American forces turned east down the coast road; they were mightily aided in capturing the successive ridges by the gunfire of our cruisers, which moved along the shore shooting out each successive position from the flank.

By the 29th, Patton's men were everywhere in contact with the main Axis line of resistance. On August 1 the 1st Division attacked the central mountain ridges at Troina, while the British, who had been making little progress in extremely hard fighting toward Catania, attacked by the left with the Canadians carrying the weight of the drive toward Adrano in the center. The Troina position was to be typical of German defenses throughout: it was on the crest of a lofty ridge with artillery positions on the reverse slope. A deep narrow valley separated the ridge from a hill, on our side, slightly lower but still steep. Around the valley ran a mountain road which the Germans had dynamited at all precipices to make wheeled traffic impossible. Valley and road were kept under heavy observed artillery fire, to prevent repairs. The position was thickly mined and the mines covered by belts of fire from machine guns well dug in.

Against this position the American forces used light bombers in great quantity; and also artillery as fast as the engineers could get it forward, and infantry which inched through the minefields and machine-gun complex. It was the heaviest kind of fighting and the casualties were severe, but on the morning of August 4 our infantry had worked through the German line. They had to be supplied by air for a while but the structure of the defense had collapsed. That same day the Canadians broke the enemy center at Adrano.

Meanwhile at a conference between Hitler, Mussolini, and their chiefs of staff, the German generals declared that the Italian peninsula could not be held in the face of Allied air and naval power. They wanted everything abandoned up to the mountains defending the industrial Po Valley. The Nazis had remorselessly deserted their allies to gain time for themselves in Africa and Sicily. This new proposal brought about the fall of the Mussolini regime, when that first of the dictators was dismissed by his King, Victor Emmanuel. The latter brought from retirement to head the state a man of known Allied sympathies, Marshal Badoglio, who instantly entered upon a series of complex and secret negotiations looking toward transferring Italy's strength from the Axis side to ours. New orders went out on August 1 to German General Hube, who had replaced an Italian in supreme command in Sicily. He was to fight a disengaging action under cover of immense numbers of anti-aircraft guns brought over to help him. He got some 88,000 men out before August 17, when Americans and Canadians together broke into Messina.

Allied casualties had been 31,158; the point at which the weight of the fighting fell is shown by the fact that less than one third of them were American. In return, 37,000 Germans had been disposed of and Italy was knocked out, for the negotiations leading to her surrender were already in progress when Messina fell, and an armistice was signed on September 3. The Nazis had shown much tactical skill and had extricated the bulk of their forces, but they had no real answer to an Allied strategy based on domination of sea and air when the struggle was carried on in regions that could be reached by water.

TOWARD the close of July, 1943, the Combined Chiefs of Staff met in Quebec and authorized General Eisenhower to seize Sardinia and Corsica and to invade the Italian peninsula, pushing beyond Rome, where airfields were to be set up looking forward to a landing in Southern France in support of the general Continental invasion. For the attack on Italy the troop formations were again shuffled. The British Eighth Army, including the Canadians, got across the Strait of Messina on September 3 and began moving north through Calabria. German resistance to Montgomery's force was confined to demolitions and weak rear guards which always pulled out as soon as they had forced the advancing Allies to deploy. By the 8th of the month the army had reached the point where the toe of the Italian boot joins the main structure.

That night three things happened. The Italian surrender was announced. A British airborne division struck at the key naval base at Taranto. A fleet of transports moved in on the beaches of Salerno, just below Naples, carrying the new U. S. Fifth Army, a unit under the command of Mark Clark (now a Lieutenant-General), which contained one British and one American corps. It had been hoped that the conclusion of Italy's surrender might allow the Fifth Army to knife rapidly through to the north-south highways and cut off important German forces facing Montgomery, while

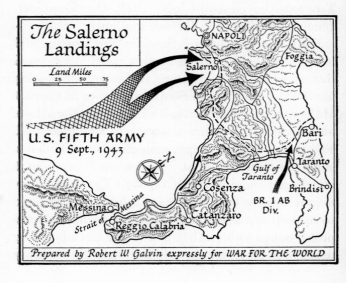

The Salerno Landings

Land Miles
0   25   50   75

U. S. FIFTH ARMY
9 Sept., 1943

NAPOLI

Foggia

Salerno

Bari

Taranto

Gulf of Taranto

Cosenza

Brindisi

BR. 1 AB Div.

Messina

Strait of Messina

Reggio Calabria

Catanzaro

Prepared by Robert W. Galvin expressly for WAR FOR THE WORLD

the airborne strike would give us easy possession not only of Taranto but of the great nexus of airfields around Foggia, some 250 miles up the east coast.

Both expectations were disappointed. The hope that the Italians would be able to contribute something toward Allied victory proved utterly baseless, even those in Rome, which contained the best troops and those most devoted to Badoglio and the King, allowing themselves to be meekly disarmed by the Germans. There was no appreciable partisan movement. German parachutists rescued Mussolini, and with him set up a rump fascist republic in the north. His son-in-law, Count Ciano, who handled much of the intrigue which led to the surrender, was captured and shot.

On the military side, the airborne force got Taranto and the Adriatic port of Brindisi without difficulty, but General Hube had anticipated both the Italian surrender and the attempt at Salerno. He had eight divisions south of Naples, mostly among the westward-facing slopes of the Apennines, with great strength in armor, since two of the divisions were armored and two were motorized, which means they had nearly as many tanks as an armored division. As soon as Salerno was definitely identified as the landing point, Hube checked the progress of the British Eighth with a local counterattack and threw his strength against General

Clark's beachhead, bringing out all the planes the dwindling Luftwaffe could muster for attacks on the ships and landing craft and adding to them a new weapon here seen for the first time—the pilotless glider bomb, radio controlled.

The attack fell on the morning of July 9th as Clark's men were pushing to the low, flat marshy plain, cut up by irrigation ditches. Nothing but infantry was ashore, the beaches were piled high with supplies, and a serious shortage was developing in landing craft, many of which had been damaged in the Sicilian invasion and had not yet returned to service. The shortage was still further aggravated by aerial and glider bomb attacks, while German artillery, from positions back in the hills where it could not be reached, shelled the critical supply areas with great effect and their tanks made several counterattacks. One entire battalion was wiped out; the defenders of the beachhead were pinned to a narrow space under constant fire. Instead of getting in the rear of the troops facing Montgomery, the Fifth Army had to call on him for a drive to extricate them.

Meanwhile the Germans themselves were not without their difficulties. The Allied air forces raided them constantly, doing particular damage along the supply routes among the gorges and bridges in which Italy is so rich. Our ships offshore laid down so heavy and accurate a fire to the extent of their range inland that German armor could neither be assembled nor moved, except by night. Under cover of this fire General Montgomery moved by his left and succeeded in joining up with the beachhead after a week of the hardest kind of fighting. That same day a British armored division which had finally reached shore drove inland from Salerno itself. General Hube was now fighting both front and flank with his line of communications parallel to his front, always a dangerous situation. He made a fighting retreat, drawing his left back through the mountains.

His move was a success in one sense, since he got most of his troops out and had inflicted the heavier casualties. But now Alexander rapidly switched the British Eighth through the mountain passes toward the Adriatic, where they joined the force coming up from Taranto, and on September 27 captured the great Foggia airfields. Next day Naples fell to an American advance along the coast. The Germans had destroyed the water supply and all public utilities and choked the harbor with sunken ships, many of them concreted in. The necessity of caring for the civilian population, many of whom died of malnutrition and disease, proved a severe drag on operations later, and it was midwinter before salvage units could get the harbor into even passable operating condition. A time bomb planted in the Naples post office killed many civilians.

THE Germans had been driven back and we held the Foggia fields but the operation could hardly be called an outstanding success; American losses were heavier than for the whole conquest of Sicily, while the Germans had gained some quantity of a commodity they most needed—time. This time was used to construct a line of formal defenses along a system of mountain peaks with a stream running through, the Garigliano; another stand was made on the broad Volturno plain, south of Naples, intensely cultivated and flat, with an unfordable river running through it.

The attack on this Volturno position was mainly an American affair and had three elements. An expeditionary force was launched onto the beaches north of the Volturno mouth and a direct crossing was attempted on the lower reaches of the river. An attack was made on Capua, astride the stream, where the bridges were still intact, the over-all plan being to get around the enemy's two flanks next to the sea and the mountains. The assault began on the night of October 12–13, 1943. Both the beach landing and the crossing of the river succeeded, but the Germans were able to hold the advance within narrow bridgeheads. At Capua they counter-attacked with a considerable force of armor, got through into our rear areas where they caused confusion, then retreated by a circuit to their own lines. This involved the abandonment of the town;

on the 16th the Nazis once more made a fighting retreat out of the plain back into the mountains and the Garigliano position.

The British Eighth was supposed to move forward through the mountains near the Adriatic to keep pace with the Fifth, but just as the advance was to start a minor German bombing raid on the port of Bari set fire to a big ammunition ship; it blew up, destroying every vessel in the harbor and all the supplies for the move. Later in the month Montgomery's forces got going again in a series of local attacks that carried forward a few hundred yards a day through Nazi machine-gun positions, extensive minefields, and demolitions so thorough that the country was left incapable of supporting life. On November 20, the Eighth reached the line of the Sangro River, where a position had been fortified as a prolongation of the Garigliano line westward.

On the Fifth Army's front the Garigliano sweeps around a great boss of hills, pinching the Appian Way (coast road) close against the sea, and the only practicable road northward plunges inland to go north through a gap at the hill town of Cassino. The armies locked at this point. The Germans had somewhat the superior force in Italy—14 divisions south of Rome with 10 more in reserve behind, against 11 divisions on the Allied side. But they were kept from using all their forces by the successful deception of appointing General Patton to lead a nonexistent Seventh Army with headquarters in Corsica, which made the enemy think an invasion of the Riviera was imminent. General Alexander also had the advantage of his air force, which from the Foggia base was now giving close support and cutting up all transportation in the German rear. He decided the Nazi defense line could be broken in spite of the winter weather with heavy rains and cold.

On November 24 the British Eighth tried an attack which was beaten back with loss. On December 1 an attack near Cassino gained some ground but it was stopped before the defense position became compromised. On December 6 the Eighth Army tried again and got across the Sangro but could make nothing of the peaks beyond. On December 1, in an attack against the Garigliano line, French troops came into play. But all advances were slow and costly. The front had settled down into an approximation of the trench warfare conditions of 1916, a struggle of attrition with no end in sight.

That this was satisfactory to the Germans, who were concentrating their attention on the effort to give some stability to the immense Russian front, is only one of the reasons why the campaign had to be counted as less than a full success for the Western Allies. Their advantage clearly lay in a

war of open maneuver where the great strength of
the air arm could be used to the utmost and, above
all, where they could employ the general speed of
movement conferred by the excellent American
automotive equipment, such as the little cross-
country truck called the jeep. In spite of armor
and self-propelled guns, the German army was a
comparatively sluggish organization, with a high
proportion of horse-drawn transport and marching
infantry. For the type of fighting encountered in
Italy this did not matter; only specialized mountain troops could have done better, and the Germans had some of these, while the single division
earmarked for such use by the American army was
still in training. But in the long run, it was neither
the lack of special troops nor of supplies that delayed matters in Italy, nor was it the fact that
formations were constantly drained away for the
coming invasion of France. These factors all had
their influence, and are not to be neglected; but
the high command must bear the responsibility as
it would have gained the glory of success. The fact
is that General Montgomery was always slow in
his movements, often to the point that Eisenhower
and Alexander became much irritated with him;
and General Clark, though an extremely able staff
officer and a priceless negotiator, was even slower,
and quite lacking in the strategic sense and driving
ability Montgomery so richly had. In a defensive

situation he might have been adequate; but in this campaign, where attacks were desired, it would probably have been better to relieve him. But the Italian front had already become secondary by October in the estimation of our leaders. General Eisenhower was back in London preparing for the invasion of France, and almost as fast as divisions obtained a degree of combat experience in the mountains, they were withdrawn to England to be the nucleus formations of the main effort.

CHAPTER VIII

SEA AND AIR

1943

ONE of the reasons for the slowing up of the Allied drive in the Mediterranean basin, and the failure to land elsewhere then in Italy, was the lack of means in the form of shipping. This was both a shortage of ocean-going bottoms and of shallow-draft craft for beachhead purposes. The two were not unconnected; both were fundamentally due to the German U-boat war, which in the course of 1942 had destroyed 1,161 Allied merchant vessels. Every effort was made to spread construction of landing craft among minor shipyards and inland industrial establishments, serving assembly slips along the coast with prefabricated parts, in order to leave the major shipyards free for the construction of ocean-going tonnage; but difficulties were encountered at two levels. A shortage existed in the basic steels of which all ships are made and a special shortage in propulsive machinery, the production of which admitted no easy solution along the lines of prefabrication.

These difficulties were reflected in the program for building the ships most useful for combating submarines. As early as 1941 the navy had prepared a design for a vessel it called the "destroyer escort," about the size of a destroyer of the previous war but with less complex engines, though still with speed enough to enable it to overtake a large fast submarine on the surface. (The British-built corvettes were based on trawler design and were so lacking in speed as to be restricted to the defensive.) More than 500 destroyer escorts were ordered and many were in the water by the end of 1942, but they were withheld from active service by lack of machine parts.

Early in 1943 this difficulty began to be solved. Destroyer escorts were appearing at the rate of twenty to thirty a month, armed with radar and the hedgehog, a device which projected a spread of small depth charges over the bows after the manner of a shotgun. These charges had the inestimable advantage of exploding only on contact with the submarine, so that sound-locating devices did not lose track of the enemy during the course of an action.

The light submarine chasers and the accumulation of shore-based aircraft had already driven the

U-boats from the east coastal waters of the United States in 1942; by June of 1943 destroyer escorts and heavy patrol planes had made operations in the Caribbean and Gulf of Mexico unprofitable to the raiders. In any case the military situation had now made it more important to the Germans to interrupt the transatlantic traffic in troops and arms than to engage in more generalized forms of reducing Allied tonnage.

The enemy's retort was both tactical and strategic. Strategically the Germans shifted the weight of their submarine war to two areas, the South Atlantic and the middle reaches of the North Atlantic, where convoys were beyond reach of cover from land-based aviation. Tactically they brought into operation a method known as the "wolf pack" technique. It had been earlier shadowed forth, especially during the winter campaign in the Caribbean, when submarines often worked in pairs. As fully developed, a group of U-boats all the way up to ten in number would string out in a patrol line across a region of ocean, assembling round a convoy at a distance too great to be attacked by its escorts. The U-boats on the surface had more than twice the speed of the convoy. At night they would close in and attack, often on the surface, always simultaneously. These mass attacks frequently resulted in the loss of one or more submarines. They nearly always cost us several ships; and, including its cargo, a single ship was probably more valuable than a submarine.

In the South Atlantic these methods produced an actual food shortage for a time along the northern coast of Brazil, which is served wholly by water, but the chief result was to bring that nation wholeheartedly into the war. So efficient a system of air scouts and striking groups was set up by Vice-Admiral Jonas Ingram, who commanded the Brazilian forces as well as our own, that by October, 1943, fifteen of the eighteen submarines that entered the area had been sunk and the Germans gave up the operation. In the North Atlantic the wolf-pack method had hardly been begun before the Allied reply was at hand.

As early as January, 1940, the American navy had launched a small aircraft carrier by building a flight deck on supporting struts over the hull of a merchant vessel. This vessel, the escort carrier *Long Island*, went through a long period of experimentation, for there was grave doubt over her ability to launch or take in planes, since the 16–19 knot speed of a fast commercial craft is well below the 27 knots of a slow carrier. The technical difficulties were overcome in time for *Long Island* to furnish the air cover and scouting for the battleship squadron that stood in reserve at Midway. In the meantime 16 similar conversions had been begun on standardized and therefore rapidly pro-

duced fast freighter hulls for British account before
Pearl Harbor. On that date our ally already had
five in service and was using them to cover important convoys. One was torpedoed at the entrance
of the Mediterranean during the African invasion.
By the summer of 1943 the tactics and methods of
handling these craft were well worked out and more
than 75 were building. By September, when *Bogue*,
the first to operate under the American flag in the
Atlantic, appeared, these awkward-looking vessels
under British colors were already a familiar sight
to the men of the troop convoys.

They had manifest disadvantages. The ships
were cranky, the number of planes they could
handle was small, they were difficult to maneuver
in a seaway and so slow that, when they turned into
the wind to launch planes, a convoy often got so far
ahead that the carriers could not catch up. But,
flying planes from the very region of a convoy,
these ships kept the wolf packs at such a distance
that it was often impossible for them to close in
for night attacks, and in the daytime they forced
the U-boats underwater and altogether prevented
any attack, since a submarine's underwater speed
is low. Teamed with destroyer escorts they even
counterattacked the U-boats, planes from the escort carriers spotting and bombing the submarines,
whereupon the surface ships moved in with hedgehog and depth charges. One "hunter-killer group"

centering on the escort carrier *Card* thus disposed of no less than 11 submarines.

This group, which contained the old destroyers *Barry*, *Goff*, and *Borie*, had a famous battle with one group of large submarines in heavy weather during the early spring. One U-boat was bombed and sunk by the carrier's planes and another forced to the surface, where she was attacked by *Borie*, which rammed her. The destroyer's back was broken and she began to flood; she engaged the submarine in a furious gun duel at ranges so short that shotguns, pistols, and even knives came into play, and sent her down just before the destroyer herself foundered, her crew being rescued with difficulty by the other two. In a not dissimilar action off the coast of Africa, the men of the destroyer escort *Pillsbury* actually captured *U-505* by boarding in the manner of the days of sail; and the Coast Guard cutter *Campbell* sank another submarine in high, icy seas after an all-night duel that left the cutter herself so damaged that she reached port only with difficulty.

With the utmost persistence, groups of German submarines harassed every important transatlantic convoy, so that our ships had literally to fight their way through; and twice, at least, the Nazis torpedoed transports which went down with great loss of life. But they made the strategic error of attempting to direct all operations from Berlin via

radio, which often enabled the Anglo-American
forces to locate submarines before they could deliver an attack. They also committed the tactical
error of placing several submarines with comparatively ill-trained crews under the command of an
experienced division leader, with the idea that all
could be brought up to the standard of the latter.

By the summer of 1943 the Germans decided
that in the face of such opposition the U-boat war
could not be run on the old lines and issued orders
that, instead of submerging when attacked by aircraft, the raiders were to surface and fight it out.
During June many submarines were recalled and
fitted with heavy anti-aircraft armament. The
U-boats were out in greater numbers than ever
during the next two months with a new type of
acoustic torpedo which homed on the target ship's
propellers, and there was violent air fighting all
along the corridors of the Atlantic. Many aircraft,
both shore and carrier-based, were shot down and
a few escort vessels were torpedoed, while merchant
sinkings continued to rise week by week till November. But in September it was possible for the
Allied High Command to announce that 90 submarines had been sunk in as many days. There
were signs of declining morale in the U-boat service
and by the end of the year the new tonnage constructed was running well ahead of the losses.

PART of this gain, though as yet a small part, was attributable to the activities of the Allied bomber command. Even as the movement to Africa began, the depredations of the U-boats had become so serious that the Combined Chiefs of Staff decided that the counterattack on submarines must be given top priority in every operation that could at all affect the sea campaign. This meant primarily the bomber commands, British and American, which had been concentrating on Nazi production facilities, especially in France. The last raids undertaken by the Eighth U. S. Army Air Force, before most of its strength was sent south toward the end of 1942, were on the submarine pens at St. Nazaire, a main U-boat base. These were attacked again and again throughout the winter, while the British night bombers concentrated on the submarine bases at North Germany and Norway, which they could reach more readily since they made the long flight over enemy territory in the dark.

The submarine pens were on the waterfront and were roofed with 12 feet of reinforced concrete. They were hit frequently with considerable apparent damage to supporting installations such as rail lines and barracks, but the records show that the actual damage was small. The Germans sought by every device to give the impression that the bombings caused them more serious difficulties than was actually the case, however, since the positions of the bases both at St. Nazaire and Brest afforded admirable opportunities to bring the big bombers under anti-aircraft fire. They moved in more and more guns; by the close of December, 1942, anti-aircraft fire at both places was dangerously accurate at levels of about 20,000 feet, and though few of the big bombers were shot down, many were damaged, with resultant increased pressure on repair facilities, it having been discovered that the provision for spare parts was altogether inadequate.

New planes arrived slowly to build up the Eighth Bomber Command during the early months of 1943, and missions over Germany began to be undertaken. On January 27, a group of 53 bombers attacked a submarine base at Wilhelmshaven, and on March 5 the first raid to interior Germany was flown against the railroad yards at Hamm. Later in March the fullest force the Eighth could assemble—97 big bombers, one third of them Liberators—attacked the submarine-building yards at Vegesack and succeeded in knocking out the powerhouse in the first of a series of raids which were to have some strategic effect. Throughout the spring months bad weather canceled many missions and the raids flown were less important for any direct effect than for the information they afforded on the strength, disposition, and methods of the German defenses.

The true aerial campaign opened on May 14 with a 200-bomber raid whose main objective was Kiel. It was typical of the lines along which this air war developed. The day was begun with a flash raid of light bombers on the electric generating plant at Ijmuiden in Holland. The big formation struck at Kiel next, drawing in on itself most of the enemy fighter squadron of the North German command. While this action was in progress, another group of 50 bombers with heavy fighter escort struck at Courtrai, where the Germans had a network of airfields and maintained a fighter concentration. The German fighters that attacked this group had hardly reached ground for refuelling when still another bomber formation came over their coast, apparently making for Ghent, to which the few remaining German fighters that could be got into the air were rushed. The bombers then veered sharply to Antwerp where they bombed the factories almost without interference.

Throughout the summer aerial operations continued on these general lines of main attack and efforts at distraction, but with marked changes in the supporting detail. As early as June it was discovered that speed was no adequate defense for light bombers of the B-25 and B-26 types and that it was almost impossible for them to obtain surprise. They needed fighter support.

By July it was clear that the Fortresses and Lib-

erators did not team well together because of their
different flight characteristics. The latter were split
off as a separate command and toward the middle
of the summer, after an attack on Kiel which resulted in a furious air battle with considerable
losses on both sides, were withdrawn from the area.
The Foggia airfields had recently been captured.
The Liberators were based there as the nucleus of
the new 12th Air Force, where their great range
could be used in attacks on the industrial plants
of north Italy, the traffic bottleneck in the Brenner
Pass, and establishments in southern Austria.

One heavy groupment was shifted to Africa instead. After three weeks of special training it flew
across the Mediterranean and up into Rumania for
a one-blow attack on the concentration of oil wells
and refineries at Ploesti, almost the only source the
Germans had of the high-grade lubricating oils
which could not be produced synthetically. The
attack was made at roof-top level with delayed
action bombs. The place was powerfully defended
and the losses were extremely heavy, but the refineries were so badly smashed that they never
again reached full production and for many months
gave only a fractional yield.

Meanwhile in the north the air battles continued
to grow in intensity as the Germans threw a greater
and greater proportion of their aircraft-producing
capacity into fighters and armed some of these

with rockets. Fortresses in formation continued to be more than a match for normal fighter opposition, but the rocket planes would fire a salvo of these missiles into a formation, causing it to break up so that the separate planes could be attacked by normal gun fighters. By these means heavy losses were inflicted on Fortress formations over Regensburg and Schweinfurt (62 out of 228 bombers engaged) in October. But by this time it was already evident that, like lighter bombers, the Fortresses required fighter protection.

Two means of providing it were worked out. One was to give full fighter cover, a task involving great nicety of calculation, since all types of fighters paid for their high speed by an endurance much below that of the bombers. The method was to escort the bombers over the European coast and some distance inland by means of the admirable but very short-range British Spitfires. At this point, or near the target, the escort duties would be taken over by American P-47 Thunderbolts, a heavy and powerful high-altitude fighter of considerable range which began to appear in numbers during the summer. On the return journey, Spitfires would again pick up the bombers over the coast of France and see them home.

The second method was to include, in each formation, Fortresses from which the bombs had been removed in favor of a heavy load of guns and ammunition. This proved abortive since the heavily loaded fighter Fortresses could not hold speed with the rest on the home journey after the bombs had been discharged.

The Regensburg-Schweinfurt raids also marked a change in aerial strategy. The attacks on submarine pens were evidently not producing results, and those on the submarine-building yards had only led the Germans to change their system of construction to that of prefabricating entire sections of U-boats inland and treating the building yards as assembly points where these were brought together. By August the weight of air attacks was shifted to German key industries, like the various synthetic gasoline establishments and the aircraft factories.

The losses in the Schweinfurt attack (a ball-bearing plant) were too heavy, and the attempt to knock out any single key industry was abandoned. The Nazis met the attacks on their aircraft factories by dispersion and by putting the more important plants underground. German plane production, though far below the enemy's wishes and hopes, showed an increase of more than 60 percent for the year. On the other hand, toward the close of the year the attacks on oil plants began to produce results in the form of shortages that forced the enemy severely to ration this material. When it was learned that the Nazis had given locomotives and railroad cars first priority on construction materials it became evident that a somewhat unexpected transportation crisis was developing within the Reich. For a year British fighters had made a specialty of shooting up trains in France and Holland, and their big night bombers, which in the fall of 1943 still outnumbered ours by three or four to one, had devoted much attention to freight yards, canal locks, and factories for automotive equipment. In August they sent 1,000 heavy bombers to Hamburg on three successive nights. The city was not destroyed, as optimistic estimates had it at the time, but its transportation system was completely wrecked and Hamburg thenceforth became a thoroughly inefficient producer both of submarines and aircraft.

By the close of the year then, if the air war had not yet seriously hurt the enemy, the terms on which it could do so were discovered and both the strategy and tactics of daylight air operations had been thoroughly worked out. There was no longer any doubt that the American precision system of bombing was a success, not as a rival to the British "area" raids but as a supplement to them. In the fuel and transportation setup a target had been found whose further injury would shake the entire enemy structure. The aircraft and trained crews were coming forward in so widening a stream that at the turn of the year the American planes in action nearly equaled the British in numbers. Perhaps most important of all, in aerial combat over their own territory the Germans were losing planes far faster than we. They were showing a marked unwillingness to engage except under special conditions that became steadily rarer.

Some idea of the effort expended in the strategic air war can be given statistically. At the close of the war, 7,177 bombers and 6,203 fighters were operating with the American forces, with 6,956 bombers and 7,728 fighters with the British. No fewer than 9,949 American and 11,965 British bombers had been lost from all causes, but the Americans had dropped 1,461,864 tons of bombs on German territory and had destroyed 35,783 German planes; the British had dropped 1,233,609 tons of bombs and had destroyed 21,622 German fighters.

CHAPTER IX

THE country around Buna and Gona on the north coast of Papua is a tropical jungle swamp with dense vegetation. After their defeat among the Owen Stanley Mountains in the fall of 1942, some 11,000 Japanese were surrounded there, in an area about ten miles long, by troops of the Australian 6th and American 32nd divisions. It was the first campaign in history completely supplied and supported by air; weapons and food were dropped in parachutes, while men were brought in by light planes which landed on strips laboriously hacked out among the trees.

The operations of our planes had cut off nearly all supply and reinforcement from the enemy. But although they were in a hopeless position of the sort in which European troops would have made a somewhat formal resistance before coming to terms, these enemies showed no disposition whatever to save their own lives. Moreover, the whole position was found to be fortified with extraordinary skill. Pillboxes of concrete had been installed with the floor four or five feet below ground level; they were lined and roofed with coconut logs, over which earth had been piled and quick-growing tropical vegetation planted to make the structure all but invisible. Giant tree roots had been turned into machine-gun nests, and among the branches of the trees themselves there were snipers. Finally, all this system of fortifications was connected by an intricate maze of tunnels and passageways, so that as fast as the Japanese were driven from one bunker they would appear in another to open fire.

The combination presented military problems unlike anything our men had ever encountered. Mortars were nearly useless against these bunkers; the overhanging branches deflected the shells. Air bombing produced no results because of the difficulty of identifying targets in the jungle. Some light artillery was flown in, but it required a direct hit on a pillbox porthole to put the structure out of business, and this could not be obtained without observation from posts so far forward that they came under fire from other pillboxes of the system. Medium tanks could not be brought in because there were none in the South Pacific at this date, and even if there had been any, we lacked control of the sea north of New Guinea across which to move them.

Under these conditions Allied advances against the line of fortifications came almost to a standstill in mid-November, 1943. The Australians at Gona on the left did much better than the American troops, breaking into that village on the 23rd with the aid of a handful of light tanks that had been flown in partly disassembled. The Japanese held out in their pillboxes and each had to be taken separately. It was December 8 before the last of them was reduced, and by this time the American division had suffered several repulses and was so shaken that there had to be changes in command. Buna was in fact the more formidable position of the two. Even after the more experienced Australians joined the 32nd against it, the advance was by inches and the front was really stalled until the arrival of an Australian tank brigade on January 2, 1943. This broke through the periphery, but it was January 23 before resistance within the area was broken down and the last Japanese were exterminated, only 117 of them surrendering.

It had been a key campaign, whose significant feature was the failure of the defenders, despite their skill and tenacity in the face of attacks from the air against their communications.

AFTER the great sea battle off Guadalcanal in November, 1942, there was a lull on the water for a week or more while the Japanese reconsidered their position. In proportion to its total size, their army had suffered little, and their navy was materially still in excellent shape, falling behind ours chiefly because of our larger building program, which, by the way, they estimated even beyond its actual size because they persistently exaggerated our losses, and believed we were throwing in ever larger numbers of new ships. Their air forces had numerically made good all losses, and if most of their carriers were now out of action, so were most of ours. But in the broad strategic picture, the depredations of the American submarines were already causing difficulties; the program for the exploitation of the Indies was not coming off at all well, and worst of all, in a military sense, the Japanese had lost the spirit of the offensive. As strategists, they had the rather peculiar characteristic of being unable to work out sound plans without taking time to prepare everything in a minute detail that left no liberty of action whatever to tactical commanders.

As the Japanese High Command saw the matter, then, their need was time—to plan, to develop resources, to dominate our submarines as we were dominating the German submarines in the Atlantic. This time was to be gained by a dogged defense of Guadalcanal. The American forces on that island were now strong enough to begin edging forward, both inland towards the mountain keel and westward across the ridges and deep jungle-covered draws leading to the shore. The respite closed when the enemy came down the Slot with a Tokyo

Express in a new form—transports covered by strong flotillas of destroyers, of which one division would run in to cover the landing while the rest steamed round on guard in what had become known as "Iron Bottom Bay."

These forces were too strong for our small groups of PT-boats to deal with, the water was too deep for minelaying, and there were not enough American destroyers in the South Pacific to meet the enemy on their own terms. But our command continued to be notified of enemy tentatives by the system of coast watchers and air scouts, and when a convoy of eight fast Japanese transports came down on the night of November 30 under charge of six destroyers, Admiral Halsey sent Rear Admiral Carlton Wright in with a squadron of four heavy cruisers and one light. The Japanese transports were lying along the shore at Tassafaronga; their destroyers were outside. The loom of the shore and the confused mass of shipping interfered with American radar as our ships opened fire. A couple of enemy destroyers rushed close enough to fire spreads of torpedoes. The destroyers were sunk, mainly by the rapid fire of the light cruiser *Honolulu,* and our heavy cruisers destroyed every one of the Japanese transports. But their torpedoes got home: the heavy cruiser *Northampton* went down; *Minneapolis* and *New Orleans* had their bows blown off; and *Pensacola* was badly holed.

With great effort and difficulty the damaged
ships were dragged to Tulagi Harbor and camouflaged under vegetation, while repair parties worked
frantically to get them in shape to move. To the
surprise of everyone on our side the expected Japanese clean-up attack did not come. It developed
that this battle, in which the loss was so dispro-
portionately heavy on our side as to make it a
tactical defeat, was really the crowning strategic
victory of the campaign. The Japanese had been
wiped out with a loss in transports they could ill
afford; they never sent unarmed vessels down the
Slot again. Their destroyer groups continued to run
occasionally, all the way up to 22 in number, and
there was no good way of checking these. But
toward the end of the year it became clear that the
enemy was no longer bringing in new troops but
trying to take out those they already had on Guadalcanal. The American advance was now steady,
and on February 8, 1943, the last organized resistance was put down.

By this time another phase of the Solomons
campaign had already begun. Since they could
not have Guadalcanal for themselves, the Japanese
had determined to render it valueless to us by sealing it off from the upper islands of the Solomon
chain and keeping everything that moved in the
surrounding waters under constant aerial attack.
They had developed a good forward airfield at

Munda on New Georgia and a minor one with a
supply base at Vila-Stanmore on nearby Kolombangara, as well as a seaplane base at Rekata Bay
on Santa Isabel; this was a major base for both
planes and ships among the Shortland Islands at
the foot of Bougainville and was supported by
only slightly less formidable installations at Kieta
and in the Buin-Faisi area of Bougainville. The
whole complex led out of Rabaul, which had been
built up till it was the major Japanese base in
the Southwest Pacific, more important than Truk.

The new system was accompanied by a strategy
and tactic which were unveiled in the last days of
January. A Japanese battle fleet from Truk allowed itself to be scouted by our planes and submarines, as it moved down toward the Solomons
in great strength. Admiral Halsey's reply was to
move his own heavy battle squadron up into supporting position and to institute a cruiser patrol
under Rear-Admiral Giffen on a line from the New
Hebrides up toward Guadalcanal.

The patrol consisted of three heavy cruisers
under Giffen's personal command and the three
new light cruisers of the *Cleveland* class, first of
the war-built ships to join the fleet, under Rear-
Admiral A. S. Merrill. The evening of January 29
found them steaming toward Rennell Island. As
twilight fell, a Japanese snooper plane swept past,
outlining the squadron with floating flares of a new

type. The ships were instantly rushed by 20 torpedo planes. Six were shot down; aided by the bad light and the surprise, the rest got away, after dropping their torpedoes, two of which hit the heavy cruiser *Chicago*, with crippling damage.

There was every chance that the Japanese would send in a concentration to finish off their victim. Halsey ordered Giffen to drop *Chicago* behind under cover of some of his destroyers while clearing the area with his other ships. The next noon the attack came—more torpedo planes. Nearly all were shot down but they hit *Chicago* twice more and she sank. The operation could be counted a distinct Japanese victory, for the cost in planes was small beside the value of the lost cruiser.

The teasing advance of the Japanese fleet was not a trick that could be worked indefinitely, however, nor were twilight torpedo attacks so effective after this one, for night-firing arrangements in the American fleet were improved. On February 18, when the Japanese attempted the same method against a convoy moving in under guard of a division of destroyers under Captain L. A. Abercrombie, they lost six of their bombers for no return at all; while a day or two earlier Rear-Admiral W. H. Ainsworth had moved in with a division of light cruisers to give the torpedo plane base at Munda a shelling that smashed a number of planes and left nearly 5,000 dead in the barracks area.

On February 19, a heavily armed and escorted expedition took the first step forward from Guadalcanal—to the Russell Islands, which were found unoccupied. Work was begun at once on the new air strip and a PT base. This marked the opening of a new phase in the Solomons campaign. The American air forces dominated most of the Solomons area during daylight, running continual raids as far up as the Shortlands, which was the practical limit of range for escorted bombers. At twilight the enemy planes came out, many times attempting to repeat their coup of Rennell Island, and all night their bombers made hit-and-run raids on points that looked promising, nor had our forces any night fighters to drive them off. Now and again they would stage a major airstrike by day, as on April 7, when over a hundred bombers came down on a big convoy off Guadalcanal, sinking a destroyer and a tanker.

Underneath this aerial bickering the American forces were assembling for a push up the Solomons chain. A new division of army troops was gradually brought in (shipping was still the shortage) and fresh forces of Marines. It would have to be a campaign of very much limited liability this time, the naval support restricted to Ainsworth's division of three light cruisers and Merrill's of four, with a battleship force in the offing but not to be used in the narrow and submarine-infested waters save in reply to a threat from the enemy's heavy ships or for absolutely necessary major bombardment.

THE reason for this sudden shortage of naval support in what had been one of the most crucial areas of the war was that the Battle of Guadalcanal set the American fleet free to attempt operations elsewhere. Already in January of 1943 it had been understood that Admiral Giffen and his heavy cruisers were to remain in the south only until clearing weather permitted an expedition to recover the outer Aleutians. After the attack on Dutch Harbor of July, 1942, American strength had been built up rapidly in that previously neglected area. The perpetual fogs that afflict the islands made it an air and submarine affair through 1942 and most of the winter, with a constant exchange of raids, but with the American forces gradually gaining through superior technology.

In the earliest phase our heavy seaplanes of the PBY type were used as dive bombers against Kiska, coming down through the fog to the area of visibility close along the surface. The Japanese attempted to defend by means of float seaplanes, but had no effective method of counterattack, as their machines had insufficient range. The American bombings did little to destroy their construction work, but a good many Japanese ships were damaged and this effect was accentuated by the operations of our submarines, one of which worked into Kiska harbor and sank three destroyers there, of which two were later salvaged.

At the same time work was carried forward in the face of almost incredible difficulties on a new landing field at Adak, far down the chain. By mid-September army heavy bombers with fighter escort were operating from that point, attacking both Kiska and Attu whenever the fogs cleared enough to give them visibility for bombing. This procedure soon made it difficult for the enemy to use surface shipping in supplying these new bases; the bombers normally found the harbor empty. But the Japanese continued to run supplies in by submarine, and there was no cessation in their process of hacking out an air strip by hand labor. In the meanwhile American forces had taken another jump forward to establish an air strip on Amchitka, a low swampy island only 70 miles from Kiska. In February as this strip began operations, it was discovered that the Japanese were already well forward with a new and larger strip on Attu.

The indication was that they intended to convert the Aleutian theater from a diversionary effort into a field of serious operations. Our surface patrols in the area were being handled by a division of 25-year-old light cruisers supported by a single heavy cruiser. Toward the end of March, Rear-

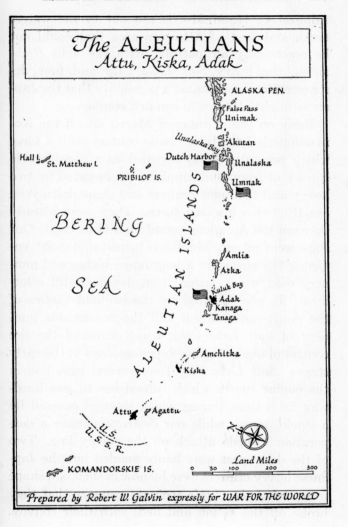

The ALEUTIANS
Attu, Kiska, Adak

ALASKA PEN.

False Pass
Unimak

Unalaska Bay
Akutan

Dutch Harbor
Unalaska

Hall I. St. Matthew I.

PRIBILOF IS.

Umnak

BERING

SEA

Amliæ

Atka

Kuluk Bay
Adak
Kanaga
Tanaga

ALEUTIAN ISLANDS

Amchitka

Kiska

Attu Agattu

U.S.
U.S.S.R.

KOMANDORSKIE IS.

Land Miles

0   50   100   200   300

Prepared by Robert W. Galvin expressly for WAR FOR THE WORLD

Admiral C. H. McMorris ran out to the waters north and west of Attu (an area that could not be reached by air patrols) with the light *Richmond,* the heavy *Salt Lake City* and four destroyers, to cover against a possibility that the Japanese might attempt to run in a convoy.

Early on the morning of March 26, off the Komandorskie Islands, he made contact with a force which presently stood revealed as a considerable convoy of troop and supply ships, escorted by two heavy and two light cruisers and eight destroyers, exactly twice his own force. They were already between the American squadron and its base. Our ships were cut off. McMorris turned southwest, engaging the enemy in a long-range high-speed gunnery duel which lasted from daybreak till afternoon. It was featured by the brilliant tactics of the American Admiral and the remarkable gunnery of *Salt Lake City,* which wrecked the fire control of one of the big Japanese ships in the early stages. *Salt Lake City* took several hits, one in the engine spaces which caused her to lose headway for a time, during which she was covered by a smoke screen while our destroyers made a desperation torpedo attack on the enemy line. Two of the destroyers were badly mauled but the Japanese heavy cruisers were by now in such bad shape from *Salt Lake City's* accurate gunnery that they broke off the action and fled, with their convoy.

This was the last Japanese attempt to reinforce their conquest in the north. As at Buna, they found the problem of communications insoluble. They still had the same defensive devices as in New Guinea, however; and against these defenses Admiral Giffen brought up his forces in May. He had not only his cruiser squadron but three of the older battleships, an escort carrier, and a full division of troops. (By an inexcusable blunder the 7th Division had been selected, a command trained and equipped especially for desert warfare.) The landing on Attu was made without difficulty on May 11 under cover of naval gunfire; but as the troops advanced inland they encountered positions of the same general type as in New Guinea, deeply dug in and well camouflaged, with interlocking fields of fire. Casualties were severe, the division commander proved incompetent and had to be removed in the midst of action. When the Japanese positions were broken into, they closed the campaign with a mass suicidal charge in which they entered the American hospital area to kill wounded, sick, and doctors. Only 11 prisoners were taken from the 2,000 Japanese on the island.

The suicide charge occurred on May 30. It was August 15 before sufficient forces could be assembled for the attack on the much more important positions at Kiska, estimated to be held by over 10,000 Japanese. The place had been subjected to violent bombing and shelling, the planes drawing some reply from anti-aircraft fire to the last day; but when landing parties were thrown on the beach Kiska was found completely evacuated. As a whole, the campaign reflected no great credit on American arms; but the engineering achievements and the Battle of the Komandorskies were decisive. By winter of 1943 heavy bombers were taking off from Adak and Amchitka to strike at Paramushiru and the northward prolongation of the Japanese home island chain.

IN MOVING into the Central Solomons in the summer of 1943, Admiral Halsey had a small force of Marines with the 25th and 43rd Army Divisions. The installations centering around Munda airfield were chosen as a point of attack. Reef, shoal, and swamp made it impossible to land on the foreshore of the airfield itself. The plan was accordingly to seize a foothold on Rendova Island across Blanche Channel and use it for artillery support, while a striking force landed on New Georgia for an overland attack from the east and another smaller party landed on the shore of Kula Gulf and set up a road block on the barge-and-overland route by which Munda was supported from Vila-Stanmore.

Japanese scouts spotted the assembly of transports at Guadalcanal and on June 16 they threw in a heavy daylight air raid with formations staged

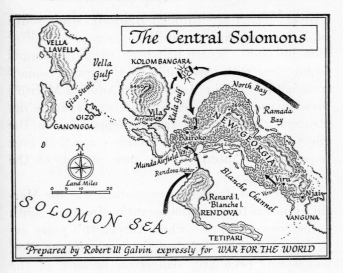

The Central Solomons

Prepared by Robert W. Galvin expressly for WAR FOR THE WORLD

all the way down from interior China. They achieved nothing, and lost 107 planes in a great air battle on that date. Two weeks later the expeditionary forces struck. Rendova was taken easily, and part of the 43rd got ashore inside Blanche Channel. The Japanese made repeated small counterattacks by air all day long and got one big transport in the process, but lost a good many planes and did not delay the landings. The flanking force also landed promptly, but here we lost a destroyer to a Japanese submarine during the operation.

As soon as the land fighting started, the Japanese began reinforcing by means of troop-carrying destroyers which ran through Blackett Strait south of Kolombangara to put their cargoes ashore at Vila by night. There had been several attempts to interfere with this traffic by the cruiser squadrons, notably one in March, when Admiral Merrill's division caught and despatched two Japanese destroyers. Now as the traffic stepped up in the effort to defend Munda, it became more than ever important to interrupt this new version of the Tokyo Express.

The general strategic arrangement was for Merrill's cruisers to cover the operation from the south —the seaward flank—while Ainsworth's more experienced division handled the work up the Slot, which was peculiarly dangerous because of the narrow waters and the certainty that any ships found there by daylight would be subjected to violent aerial attack. On July 5 there were indications that the Japanese would run a strong force in. Ainsworth took his division up the Slot and just after midnight encountered the enemy at the entrance to Kula Gulf, from which the battle takes its name—an action fought at high speeds in pitch darkness and amid considerable confusion. The fine cruiser *Helena*, which had participated in nearly all the battles for Guadalcanal, was torpedoed and went down; the Japanese lost two of their big new cruiser-destroyers.

Meanwhile the land campaign went badly. The

flanking force on the Kula Gulf side got its road block set up but could not advance beyond that point and had to be supplied chiefly from the air. The main attack encountered a complex of the same type of position that had been found at Buna, but here even more heavily fortified and armed with guns that made attack by light tanks useless. The campaign stalled in advances of a few yards a day, some of which were lost to counterattacks. The 43rd had to reorganize and reinforcements had to be sent in.

When *Helena* went down, several hundred survivors got on to wreckage and life rafts, which managed to keep together while drifting along the current of the Slot past Kolombangara to ground on Vella Lavella Island, where they notified the Guadalcanal base of their presence through the radio of a New Zealand coast watcher. Admiral R. K. Turner considered it of great importance to rescue these men, and on the night of July 11 Ainsworth again took his cruiser division up for that purpose. The same night the Japanese had chosen to run another Tokyo Express. It met Ainsworth's division at the entrance of Kula Gulf in the second action of that name, another rapid and confused battle in the dark.

American gunfire, opened by radar before the Japanese were aware of the presence of our ships, was destructive. The enemy lost a light cruiser and another of their big cruiser-destroyers. But in flight they fired a torpedo barrage which gave all three of Ainsworth's ships, including the New Zealand *Leander* (which had replaced *Helena*) crippling damage and sank the destroyer *Gwin*. In the morning as the crippled vessels were making off at slow speed, the Japanese sent down every available plane to finish them off. But Admiral Turner had sent out the Guadalcanal fighters and there was a fierce air battle in which some 30 of the enemy were shot down while none got near the cruisers. A few days later the *Helena* survivors were rescued in an elaborate operation by several divisions of destroyers.

THE two Kula Gulf battles were generally favorable to our side in spite of the damage, for the Japanese ceased trying to support Munda, leaving the men there to fight till they were killed, which result was substantially accomplished by August 5, 1943. The very next night they attempted to run a group of one heavy and three light destroyers through Vella Gulf and Blackett Strait to Vila, in anticipation that the Americans would lay siege to that place as the next in the chain. The move had been expected. The vessels were met by Commander Frederick Moosbrugger with a division of six destroyers, and the enemy's own tactics were turned against him by firing torpedoes in the dark before engaging with the guns. It was a complete victory; the enemy heavy and two of his light destroyers went down, the survivor escaping only with difficulty and heavy damage.

A new strategic situation was now presented to the American command. In the north, the operation in the Aleutians was in full progress and, in Europe, that against Sicily. Both were making heavy demands for cruiser and destroyer support and, with the incapacitation of Ainsworth's ships, Merrill's was the only squadron that could be spared for operations in the Solomons. Involvement in such another siege as that of Munda, with the necessity of providing gunnery support and intercepting Japanese efforts at relief would be almost certain to produce damage to ships, whereas experience indicated that the Japanese island bases were powerless if we possessed airfields close enough to them to cut their communications. The next step therefore was not to Kolombangara for a direct attack on the Vila position, but past it to Vella Lavella Island, where the Japanese had no occupation forces to speak of.

The move was accomplished on August 15 with little fighting. On the following night the Japanese, still apparently with their minds fixed on Vila, tried to run in a big convoy of fast troop-laden barges, straight across the Slot from Choiseul Island under destroyer escort. A division of American destroyers drove off the escorts in a brief gunnery fight and sank most of the barges with enormous losses among the occupants. This was the last attempt to reinforce Vila, the enemy changing his plan to one of straight rear-guard fighting.

Under this new system, everything American that moved on the water was subjected to harassing air attacks, mainly at night and usually with torpedoes, after snooper planes had outlined the target with flares as in the attack on Admiral Giffen's squadron early in the year. The burden of the work afloat lay on the destroyer men, and in the air on the aviators working from fields newly won from jungle. All through August and September this type of fighting went on in a series of tiring daily battles too small to be recorded. The Japanese were gradually growing weaker, for their planes could not hold head against ours nor were their mechanics equal to the task of maintenance. The loss figures gradually mounted to approximately ten to one. During those two months the Japanese discovered that with American air bases on both sides of it, Vila was useless. They began to evacuate at night by fast barges across the Slot to Choiseul. PT-boats could accomplish little against these barges, which were both armored and heavily armed. The destroyers had to be used and were nearly always counterattacked from the air. Fortunately none was lost; and not over 5 percent of the estimated 40,000 Japanese on Kolombangara escaped.

The question of another step forward had been that of waiting for troops and supplies, since the men who had fought at Munda needed rest. At the end of October these needs were met, and it was determined to move into the Empress Augusta Bay area of Bougainville, which would both neutralize the network of Japanese bases in the Shortlands and place their big center at Rabaul under fighter-covered attack, rendering it untenable as a harbor. The transports moved in on the night of October 30. That same night Merrill's cruisers ran out ahead to give the airfields at Buin-Faisi a shelling, and turned back to shell the Shortlands the following dawn as a means of keeping enemy planes on the ground.

The Japanese perceived the implications of the Bougainville attack at once. However willing they might be to fight rear-guard actions in the Central Solomons, this represented a threat they could not ignore. Next night, November 1, they sent down from Rabaul a squadron of four cruisers and eight destroyers to attack our transports and installations in the bay. At midnight the squadron was intercepted by Admiral Merrill with exactly the same numerical force but considerably less strength, since two of the Japanese cruisers were heavies with stout armor and eight-inch guns.

The battle was one of the most brilliant tactical performances of the whole war. Merrill flung his destroyer divisions in two flanking attacks on the Japanese as they advanced in three columns, himself with the cruisers shuttling back and forth across the head of the enemy advance, covering his torpedo attack by gunfire. After a two-hour action the enemy turned in flight; one of their cruisers and two destroyers had been sunk and all the others were more or less damaged. Merrill had suffered serious injuries to only one destroyer, hit by a torpedo.

At daybreak before the American squadron could clear the area, some 80 Japanese bombers staged down from Rabaul to attack them, but were beaten off with heavy loss and no damage to the ships. The fighting ashore had been progressing with the same dogged slowness as at the other places where Japanese were encountered in jungle, but the enemy were without prepared positions in the Empress Augusta Bay region and had difficulty getting reinforcements and supplies to the front along the narrow trails. In spite of the fanaticism of their resistance the perimeter of the landing area was steadily extended. The danger to the Rabaul base was now acute; the Japanese brought down a squadron of six heavy cruisers with lighter units to the number of 18, which were seen entering Rabaul harbor by scouts from MacArthur's command on November 5, evidently for a thrust against the beachhead.

This was more than Merrill's little squadron could handle. Well off to the south to keep beyond range of enemy aerial observation, the veteran carrier *Saratoga* had been lying in the offing, accompanied by the first of a series of new light carriers built on cruiser hulls, the *Princeton*. Halsey sent them in against this new threat. They ran north all through the night and at daybreak flew out every plane they had. There was a heavy overcast at Rabaul but with plenty of visibility underneath it. The carrier planes came through this in a surprise attack, meeting almost no airborne opposition and, amid intense anti-aircraft fire, fell on the Japanese squadron. They had been instructed to neglect the usual technique of making sure of sinking a damaged ship in favor of damaging all the enemy ships sufficiently to keep them from making the run to Bougainville. This plan was followed to the letter. Out of all the ships in Rabaul harbor only one cruiser steamed away unhurt and one of the Japanese destroyers was sunk. The following morning our scouts found Rabaul empty, the whole fleet turned back to Truk to lick its wounds.

This did not end Japanese efforts to inflict a serious blow on the beachheads. They began staging in planes in considerable quantities, and by November 10 had so many at Rabaul as to make operations difficult for our scouts. On the morning of the 11th, Halsey sent his two carriers back in from the south, while down from the Central Pacific to the region east of Rabaul came three new carriers—*Essex, Bunker Hill, Independence*—under Rear-Admiral Montgomery, which also flew out airplanes for a strike. The weather was very bad, with fog and rain, and the results at Rabaul were by no means all that could have been hoped for. But Japanese snooper planes had traced Montgomery's attackers back to his ships and the air squadrons that should have gone to Empress Augusta Bay were flown off in a great blow against the fleet instead.

Since the outbreak of the war a vast naval-aviation training program had been in progress in America, carried on with unhurrying thoroughness in spite of the time pressure. Of the new pilots produced these new carriers had the best. The air battle that followed was less a combat than a mass execution. When our land-based planes from Vella Lavella arrived in response to calls from the fleet, they found undamaged ships and over 60 Japanese planes burning on the water. They shot down 24 more planes during the enemy's retreat, and now the planned Japanese attack at Bougainville could not be delivered. This was their last attempt at a serious effort to relieve the pressure.

THE presence of Montgomery's new carriers in the brief Rabaul raid and the shortage of cruisers that made Merrill's squadron the sole support of the Bougainville expedition were effects from the same cause. After the Kula Gulf actions and the attacks in the Aleutians in the summer of 1943, it became clear that the Japanese had no further intention of risking major fleet units in defense of outposts at the perimeter of their empire. Our chiefs therefore began to consider an offensive on an oceanic scale—one which would either force the enemy into a major battle or make him give up bases to our use.

In oceanic terms the Japanese positions in the Gilberts now formed a salient; to defend them his fleet would have to venture as far from any base where damaged ships could be repaired after an action as would our own from Pearl Harbor. The enemy would thus be forced to fight us on equal terms; and battle on any terms near equality was now ardently desired by our command. The completion of our six new battleships and the enemy's losses off Guadalcanal had swung the balance on the gunnery line heavily in the direction of the American fleet, and the Japanese carrier force was known to have been cut to pieces.

There remained the land-based planes of the "unsinkable carriers" of the islands; but the use of these, a fundamental basis of Japanese strategy, contained a fallacy. The airplane could indeed move faster than any ship; but by loading planes on carrier decks it should be possible to assemble at a chosen point of impact a force of planes sufficient to overwhelm anything the local defensive resources could send up, while the strategic mobility of the fighting planes—the ability to cover long distances—was so limited that it could be brought to a combat area by ship far more quickly than it could be flown in. One of the defects of the Japanese air campaign for Guadalcanal had been precisely that their policy of piecemeal reinforcement had brought them nothing but piecemeal losses.

The date of the new campaign thus had to be set for a time when we would have carrier strength sufficient to break the local air forces in the Gilberts; and that date was set for the last days of November. At that time three large and some seven light carriers should be assembled with eight or nine escort carriers, which were now flowing from the yards at the rate of three or four a month. They were organized in groups like Montgomery's, each a semi-autonomous organization with gunnery ships in support. The force of fast battleships cruised with the whole. The old slow battleships were to furnish gunnery support at the beaches, keeping the escort carriers under guard while these latter gave close support to the troops ashore. The troops of the 27th Army Division were to fall on Makin Island while the 2nd Marine Division was assigned the island of Tarawa. Nearly three months of special training was given these landing forces.

Preliminary bombardments were begun several days before landing time, and the island was combed both with shells and gunfire for every defensive installation that had been revealed by a careful study of aerial photographs. On November 20 the double attack started with extensive use of the new types of landing vessels, for the first time in the Pacific.

At Makin a preliminary bombardment had achieved everything that could be desired. The 300 defenders left alive were stunned by shellfire and made but poor resistance. But Tarawa was more difficult. It had been fortified to an extent unrevealed by the photographs, with enormous and deep concrete dugouts roofed in steel, which resisted all bombardment. An error had been made in the preliminary timetable so that fire from the ships was lifted 40 minutes before the Marines reached the beaches, and the Japanese were given the opportunity to come out of their dugouts into firing positions. Inaccurate preliminary information from former residents about the height of the offshore reef at the prevailing tide had the result that many of the landing craft hung on it, under fire and losing heavily. By twilight of the first day the Marines were clinging desperately to a single small strip of

beach and part of a ruined pier. It seemed not unlikely that they would be thrown back into the sea.

Under the personal leadership of Major-General
Holland Smith they pressed on nevertheless, while
destroyers came inshore to give fire support, and
planes from all the carriers lent their aid. The
concrete bunkers proved impervious alike to shells
and bombs. The island had to be taken inch by
inch, each bunker carried in a separate military
operation by means of flame throwers, grenades,
and explosive charges. The conquest took four days
and the casualties were over 2,900, more than a
quarter of the Marines engaged. On the last day
of the fighting ashore an escort carrier in the offing
was torpedoed by a Japanese submarine, and blew
up with nearly all hands.

A thrill of horror went through the country as
this news from the Pacific followed so closely on
that of desperate fighting in Italy for results that
bulked so small on the map. The Russian counteroffensive seemed stalled; among the Solomons a
new cruiser division had appeared to join Merrill's,
but two of its ships were hit by Japanese torpedo
planes on the first night patrol, and it seemed that
the Allies like the Axis might be unable to drive
an offensive home without ruinous cost.

CHAPTER X

THE ISLAND CHAIN BROKEN

THE last Japanese troops at Buna and Gona were exterminated in January, 1943. At this time the enemy were still convinced that they could defend their empire with a hard crust of positions around its borders, using airplanes as the binding material and making a campaign as toilsome as that for Guadalcanal necessary for the capture of each position. They themselves expected to avoid their former error of wasting their mobile sea forces in the defense.

There was some reason in their viewpoint. It had taken us six months to gain control of that bloody Solomon Island, and it was only an isolated outpost, whereas the new network of positions in the south ran in a great semicircle of mutual support from Lae and Salamaua on Huon Gulf of New Guinea through New Britain down to the Munda-Vila complex in the Central Solomons. The planes from its fields made impossible any American naval effort in the sea thus enclosed.

While General MacArthur's men were laboriously consolidating the Buna-Gona position by means of men and materials taken forward by air and while Admiral Halsey's forces were preparing for their step forward into the Russell Islands, the Japanese were reinforcing the bases from which they hoped to seal off our gains. We have seen how they moved forces into the Central Solomons. At the same time they decided to put enough troops into Lae, Salamaua, and Finschaffen to make them secure against anything but an attack of the most serious character. These bases controlled Vitiaz Strait and hence access to the waters north of New Guinea.

A convoy of not less than twelve large and fast transports was assembled at Rabaul with something like two full divisions of troops aboard and a division of big destroyers for escort. On March 1, when the weather presented a favorable opportunity, with a heavy cloud and storm front running down the latitudes toward New Guinea, the expedition put out.

The preparations had been no secret from our side; in fact, one of our submarines sank a destroyer of the escort while the convoy was gathering. General George C. Kenney, commander of MacArthur's air force, had all his planes ready—somewhere around 100 of the heavy bombers which could operate at so great a distance from base. He had lately discovered that a bomb dropped by such a plane while in level flight low over the water would skip like a stone skimmed across a pond, and had been training his fliers to use this as a bombing method. As soon as the convoy was well at sea he threw his entire force upon it. The Japanese had some fighter cover but these planes were gravely hampered by the weather and still more by the tactics of the Americans, since a fighter attempting to dive upon a bomber which is at wave-top level almost invariably crashes in the sea.

The new skip-bombing technique succeeded even beyond expectations, especially since the ships practiced the normal tactic of swinging broadside to the direction of the attack to prevent the bombers running the length of their decks. Five-hundred-pound bombs plunged right in through the thin sides of transports and escorting vessels alike, exploding in the engine rooms and along the water line. By the close of the first day several ships had gone down and one had beached herself on the coast of New Britain. The rest scattered and pressed on in accordance with the Japanese doctrine of never abandoning an operation once begun, but the following morning the bombers were after them again and on March 3 were still hammering those that remained. Not one of the Japanese ships reached port, and scarcely a man ever got to shore. The disaster was so complete that General MacArthur afterward called it the decisive battle of the whole Pacific war. While it hardly merits that description, the clash in the Bismarck Sea certainly exercised a severe restrictive influence on Japanese strategy from this point forward. Never again did they attempt to move bodies of troops across open water in regions where our air power could be brought to bear.

As soon as this fact was apprehended, American South Pacific strategy was greatly simplified. It was not necessary to conduct a full campaign against each of the Japanese strong points. For an advance toward the sources of their power, it was only necessary to seize similar points among the islands ourselves and from the airfields installed at these places to provide cover for traffic moving by sea. The enemy installations could be neglected; the men in them might continue to exist on the "bounty of the tropics," but without air or sea assistance they could undertake no offensive operations. This was essentially the same conclusion that had been arrived at among the Solomons by a somewhat different line of reasoning. From the fact that the subsequent campaign was described as one of encirclements, it seems to have owed something to the strategy of land warfare as practiced by the great armies of Germany and Russia, with whom it had become normal practice to pene-

trate a front, then isolate an enemy groupment
to be mopped up more or less at leisure later.

The first fruit of this new strategy was the occupation of the Kiriwina and Woodlark Islands, north
of the eastern tip of New Guinea, on June 22–23;
where nothing beyond enemy signal stations was
found. The intervening time had been spent in
resting and reorganizing the troops who had fought
so hard at Buna-Gona in a slow advance westward
along the New Guinea shore from these places toward Lae and Salamaua and clearing up the aerial
situation. The Japanese apparently regarded Mac-
Arthur's forward move as even more of a menace
than the campaign in the Solomons, and they made
persistent efforts to lame it by the same means
they had used there. All through April and May
they continued their harassing air attacks and
though, as in the Solomons, their losses were severe,
it was not until the Kiriwina-Woodlark operation,
with the arrival of planes to use the air strip set
up there, that our forces could gain air cover
enough to move convoys with impunity around
the eastern capes of Papua.

In the spring of 1943 an Australian force had been
working toilsomely through the jungles of the Owen
Stanley Mountains, well westward of the Moresby-
Buna pass. By mid-August both this force and
that which had been moving along the coast were

in position for an attack on Lae and Salamaua. Heavy raids were flown against the Japanese supporting air bases at Wewak and Medang to keep enemy planes from interfering. Destroyers moved in to give gunnery support and the assault on Salamaua began on August 19. Although the Japanese resistance was not particularly strong in firepower, progress at first was slow despite the help of amphibian forces which landed on the beach south of the place.

General MacArthur accordingly made a rapid shift of strategy. A parachute force was dropped at Nadzab in the open Markham Valley northwest of Lae, where it successfully seized the airfield,

The New Guinea Campaign

Land Miles
100   200   400

To Morotai 15 Sept, 1944
30 July, 1944
Sansapor
27 May, 1944
2 July, 1944
11 May, 1944
22 April, 1944
Arare
Hollandia
Aitape
Wewak
Admiralty Is.
29 Feb, 1944
New Ireland
Bismarck Sea
Madang
Saidor
Finschhafen
Lae
Salamaua
Rabaul
26 Dec, 1943
Arawe
22 Sept, 1943
Huon Gulf
23 June 1943
Buna
Port Moresby
Kiriwina I.
Woodlark I.
22 June, 1943
Milne Bay
Cape York
CORAL SEA

Madang
Kajapit
Sattelberg
Finschhafen
Lae
Huon Gulf
Salamaua

Prepared by Robert W. Galvin expressly for WAR FOR THE WORLD

making room for an entire Australian airborne division which was quickly flown in. The whole Lae-Salamaua area was now cut off, and in the early days of September a concentric attack on the double position was launched. It broke through in all directions and both places were occupied by September 16. Once more there were scarcely any prisoners. The rather surprising feebleness of the defense was found to be due to the complete failure of the Japanese medical service in coping with tropical diseases, especially malaria and beriberi, which had so enfeebled the garrisons that they were in need of relief as far back as the date of the battle of the Bismarck Sea.

Finschaffen was immediately attacked by amphibious forces and was in our possession by October 2, but both from this point and from Lae a good many of the Japanese escaped to the mountain jungles of the Huon Peninsula, where they assembled on a high plateau called the Sattelburg. From this point they conducted operations well above the guerrilla level and the advance had to be halted until they were eliminated. But while this cleanup was going on, Halsey's forces got ashore at Empress Augusta Bay on Bougainville. A short time later the air strips there made it possible to keep American fighter planes over Rabaul. That struck the death knell of the great Japanese base; its fields were now untenable for aircraft and its harbor for shipping; and with the elimination of Rabaul the whole circle of Japanese outer defenses in the south fell apart.

Late in November the Japanese began running destroyers (a Tokyo Express in reverse) down to Kahili and the Buin-Faisi fields to evacuate the technical personnel of whom they had so few that every man was valuable. One of these groups was intercepted on the night of November 25 by Captain Arleigh Burke with the destroyers of the famous "Little Beaver" squadron off St. George's Channel, and in a hot little engagement he sank three of the six Japanese destroyers present without losing a man.

This substantially ended Japanese efforts to get men out of the Solomons, as similar previous actions had ended their efforts to move them in. The American advance now went on. On December 16 a strong force was thrown ashore at Arawe on the southern coast of New Britain itself, finding practically no opposition and speedily setting up a new forward base there. The way through Vitiaz Strait was now open; toward the end of the month the 32nd Division was landed on the north shore of Huon Peninsula and joined in eliminating the Sattelburg Japanese, who had been under heavy attack from two Australian divisions and who were beginning to break up at this time. The process was not accomplished without heavy fighting and some losses, but it was slow and difficult rather than dangerous in a military sense, as the Japanese had no prepared positions.

Harder fighting followed on December 26 when the 1st Marine Division was pushed through Vitiaz Strait to seize Long Island at its western end and to land on both sides of the Cape Gloucester Peninsula on the northern shore of New Britain. A small force had also worked through the mountains from Arawe to support this attack from the landward side. An important Japanese air station at Cape Gloucester formed the link between their air bases at Rabaul and Kavieng and one held by them at Wewak on the New Guinea coast. The place was accordingly heavily defended. Moreover, the preliminary aerial bombardment had failed to neutralize the Japanese field, though it was the heaviest air attack yet made in the Southwest Pacific—360 tons of bombs were dropped. In an air battle of considerable intensity the Japanese lost 61 planes; we lost seven, and several of our ships were hit.

On December 30 the Marines carried the airfield in a rush, but were brought up short before a hill behind an extensive swamp, where the enemy had dug themselves in around their artillery positions and had filled the trees with snipers. A ten-day battle was required to win the eminence; it was featured by the ingenuity of our engineers in getting troops across the swamp on foot bridges slung from trees.

Despite raids by American destroyers, the Japanese had been using Kavieng on New Ireland as an air base for the area ever since Rabaul came under attack from the bombers at Bougainville. The Cape Gloucester field brought both that point and Wewak under persistent fighter-covered attack and rendered any sustained operations by the enemy impossible. But the task of neutralizing the Japanese bases in the south was not really completed until February 16, 1944, when, supported by the cruisers from the Solomons, the 1st Cavalry Division was put ashore on Green Island close up to Rabaul and two weeks later on Los Negros Island in the Admiralty group.

The way was now clear for MacArthur's advance westward along the coast of New Guinea. One of his flanks was covered by the impassable jungles of the central part of the island, the other by open ocean. The Japanese might indeed bring their fleet into action across this ocean, but it was now alive with American cruiser, aerial, and submarine patrols, and our own fast striking forces hovered in the offing nearer to the central scene of action than were the Japanese from any concentration point they still had in operation. General MacArthur's strategy had thus far scored a complete success. His own losses were less than one to ten of the enemy's. He had thrown his bases so far forward that his own long-range bombers were attacking enemy posts in the Dutch Indies and he had cut off and pushed completely out of the war in their now-useless garrison posts a number of Japanese nearly equal to his entire army, some of the best troops in the empire.

These Japanese did not remain altogether quiescent; there was continual obscure fighting on a small scale along the approaches to Medang, on New Britain and Bougainville. But the ingenious American General turned even this to advantage by sending to these areas troops freshly arrived from the States or Australia to gain jungle-fighting experience under conditions in which they could be given so great a superiority in numbers, firepower, and air cover that their casualties were always light.

ONE of the reasons why it had been possible in February, 1944, to move up to the Admiralty Islands, a point seemingly caught between the great Japanese bases of Kavieng and Truk, was that the enemy was so deeply occupied elsewhere. During the Makin-Tarawa attacks our fleet had received the constant attention of Japanese torpedo planes, always coming in at twilight, partly from the fields in the Marshalls and partly from the lonely island of Nauru. During the Gilberts operation they hit one of the carriers, not sinking her indeed, but sending her back for a long period in dock. As soon as Tarawa was secure, in the early days of September, 1943, Admiral Lee ran down with the fast battleships and subjected Nauru to an intense surprise shelling that effectively ruined it as a base, since the Japanese had no means of replacing lost personnel and shop facilities without advancing their fleet.

For the Marshalls another method of neutralization was intended; they were the next point of attack on the line of the Central Pacific offensive that was to be conducted parallel with General MacArthur's movement along the coast of New Guinea. This island group was a widespread one, covering ten degrees of latitude and 15 of longitude, nearly as much as the Philippines, but the areas of land are very small, consisting of narrow coralline atolls encircling lagoons. No island is more than a mile or two wide. These lagoons make admirable sheltered harbors; the islands themselves need only to be cleared of some of their vegetation to become air strips.

The Japanese had been twenty years in the Marshall group, and reconnaissance photographs showed air strips on all the more important atolls. If the experience at Tarawa were any criterion, the places were formidably fortified. There was also a strong possibility that an attack on the Marshalls might bring the Japanese fleet out for a showdown fight. The island group did not constitute an outpost of empire that could be sacrificed in return for attrition among the attacking forces; it was part of the main imperial defensive system, linking up with the Carolines and Truk.

If the Japanese fleet came, our own would be hampered by the presence of the transports which it dared not leave, so the enemy could choose the time, place, and manner of attack. If our strength in carriers was now very great, it would be at least partly negated by the fact that from his numerous strips among the islands the enemy should be able to concentrate more land-based planes than had yet opposed any of our forward moves.

It was toward the weakening of these local air forces that the first efforts of the attackers were directed. As soon as the Tarawa air strip was prepared for use, long-range army Liberators and navy Venturas were brought in, and beginning on December 22, 1943, treated the whole Marshall group to a systematic pounding, with special attention to shops and fuel dumps. Between that date and January 30, Milli was thus visited 12 times, Jaluit 10, Kwajalein 8, Wotje 7, Maloelap 9, and Kusaie, the staging field in the Eastern Carolines, twice, all with heavy raids. At all these points lusty antiaircraft fire was encountered, but fighter opposition was comparatively light and showed a tendency to

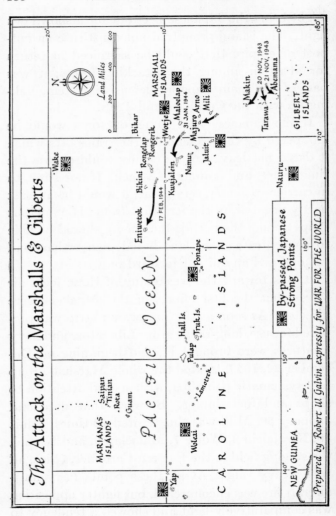

The Attack on the Marshalls & Gilberts

Prepared by Robert W. Galvin expressly for WAR FOR THE WORLD

decrease. There was no sign of any Japanese ships except submarines.

On January 30, fleet operations under the command of Admiral Spruance began with a violent simultaneous attack from the planes of three carrier groups (a carrier group normally contained two large and two small carriers, though not invariably) against the islands of Kwajalein atoll, while from escort carriers in the rear other planes joined the land-based craft. On the following morning the battleships were up and helped the planes of two carrier groups in another attack on Kwajalein which was to be the point of the landing. This was a complete surprise to the Japanese, who had expected our forces indeed, but against some atoll much farther east. Admiral F. C. Sherman's carrier group went on for a strike against Eniwetok, the most remote of the Marshalls and beyond the reach of land-based bombers from Tarawa.

Kwajalein atoll is shaped somewhat like a bent banana. At the bend is Roi, the most important island. Kwajalein Island itself is at the southern tip of the atoll. These two spots received the brunt of the attack. During the afternoon and evening of the first strike there was a good deal of air fighting around Roi but the carrier fighter group had so well disposed of Japanese scouts that local as well as strategic surprise was secured and most of their planes were destroyed on the ground. They attempted the usual torpedo-plane attacks against our fleet in the twilight but with little success, and on the morning of February 2, under gunnery cover from the old, slow battleships, the troops began to land. The 4th Marine Division attacked Roi, the 7th Army Division Kwajalein. Just after the first wave reached the shore at Roi, the battleship *Colorado* scored a direct hit on the island's main ammunition dump, which blew up with one of the most violent explosions ever seen in the Pacific.

The Japanese resisted with their usual fanaticism, but most had been stunned or killed by the explosion and what preceded it. Before night the island was American except for a few snipers. At Kwajalein the supporting fire was similarly effective and though the conquest took two days, this was mainly because it became a problem of digging the shell-shocked defenders out of the underground retreats where they had hidden themselves. Majuro atoll was occupied without resistance.

Eniwetok was scheduled to be attacked next— its possession would cut off the eastern Marshalls from Japan and would give us a valuable forward base—but the troop convoys for it were still distant and the fast carrier force of Spruance with its attack battleships was for the moment unemployed. Submarine scouts had reported heavy Japanese ships in the neighborhood of Truk. The Admiral decided to run down for an attack on that place on the chance of persuading the enemy to battle. It is not easy to convey the feeling in the fleet when the news of where they were bound spread among the ships. Truk was the Japanese Pearl Harbor, a legend and a mystery in the fleet during a generation in which no white man had been allowed to visit the place. Its strength was supposed to be immense, its defensive installations the best in the world.

Elaborate precautions were taken and elaborate tactical plans worked out, but they proved unnecessary. The Japanese fleet had fled Truk, and when our fighter planes, far in advance of the ships, swept over the great fortress on the morning of February 17 they found no major ships, but scores of Japanese fighters shooting past them into the spotty clouds to gain altitude for diving counter-attacks. There was an air battle distinguished by the fact that only fighters were engaged on both sides; the Japanese lost 127 planes shot down, we lost eighteen. Then the dive and torpedo bombers came in for attacks on the shore positions and shipping. The operation lasted two full days; on the evening of the second day a Japanese torpedo plane got a hit on an American carrier but the enemy had paid for that with 23 ships sunk, five of them warships, and the loss of 204 planes. The Truk bogey had been fully exorcised.

Spruance swung his ships back to the north and two days later raided the Marianas, where he sank more ships, mostly small, establishing the fact that the Japanese fleet was not making a wide sweep round by the north to interfere with operations in the Marshalls. Away behind Spruance the big *Saratoga* and the escort carriers had now been pounding Eniwetok for days with the help of cruiser divisions. On February 18, the same day that saw the end of the actions against Truk, Marines were set on the beaches there. The Eniwetok operation was not quite as perfect as the Kwajalein attack but came close to it. In two days the atoll was ours at the cost of 500 casualties. The whole outer barrier of Japanese defense had been broken down; Truk was effectively out of the war; and the radical defect in the Japanese system of island-based airpower had been found—that from their scattered stations the enemy could achieve nowhere near enough aerial concentration to deal with a fleet that came up out of the ocean with twenty carriers in line.

CHAPTER XI

DOMINATING the hill road through Cassino in central Italy was a monastery of great antiquity and beauty. The Germans had converted the area into a fortress and observation post which enabled their artillery, now well dug in, to come down with great accuracy on any movement from our side, while the Allied forces lacked similar aids. The position had to be won before the advance on Rome could proceed through the central valleys. For his operation of January, 1944, General Alexander planned a complex double attack to achieve the desired result.

Two British divisions were to cross the lower Garigliano and, swinging north, force the small Liri River, which flows into the Garigliano at right angles just at Cassino. The American 36th Division was to assault the line in front while a French corps was working through the mountains north of Cassino for a swing southward, similar to that being made by the British from the opposite direction. It was a double penetration to be followed by a double envelopment of the position.

Meanwhile the American VI Corps (actually only half of it was American) had been taken out of line. It would be landed from the sea on the beaches of the summer resort at Anzio-Nettuno, some thirty-five miles south of Rome. Difficulties with communications, caused chiefly by Allied aerial operations, had forced the Germans into some rather eccentric dispositions; it was hoped and expected that this triple attack would at one point or another find them unable to support a position before it could be broken through.

The British began their attack on January 17; they forced the Garigliano but were halted as they attempted to make the wheel northward. The attack of the American 36th failed under heavy losses, and though the French among the high Apennines worked through the German defensive system, no more than the British could they make the necessary wheel. The Cassino position held in spite of some local gains by the American 34th Division, which was moved into line when the 36th was driven back.

The Anzio force struck on January 22. It achieved fairly easy initial success but General Clark, in command, mindful of the difficulties at Salerno, waited for some time to get heavy equip-

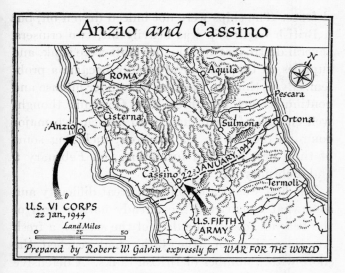

Anzio *and* Cassino

ROMA
Aquila
Pescara
Cisterna
Anzio
Sulmona
Ortona
Cassino 22   JANUARY, 1944
Termoli

U.S. VI CORPS
22 Jan., 1944
Land Miles
0   25   50

U.S. FIFTH
ARMY

Prepared by Robert W. Galvin expressly for WAR FOR THE WORLD

ment and tanks ashore, meanwhile confining his
activities to patrols. At the end of three days the
Germans had not only recovered from their surprise but also they had beaten back the 36th Division in the south and brought the British to a halt.
They rushed in all their reserves, including much
armor, cut the drainage dikes of what had once
been a system of swamps, and from dominating
hills in the rear opened a terrific fire both on the
beaches and the supporting ships. An improved
type of glider bomb was also directed at everything
that moved on the water, with the design of cutting the beachhead units from their support.

The hopeful offensive was changed to desperate

defense. The ships were not indeed driven off, but a British battleship was heavily hit, two cruisers, several destroyers and smaller craft were sunk, and supplies on the beachhead rapidly became a problem. Everything in the area was under intense and continuous artillery fire. The Germans thought well enough of their chances to launch two major counterattacks with six divisions, including some of their best armored formations, on February 9 and February 17.

The first was beaten off with great difficulty and somewhat constricted the already narrow area of the beachhead. By the date of the second, a fresh American division (the 45th) had reached the shore with a number of British tanks. A defensive perimeter was organized and held, along the lines of some canals. The Germans themselves had suffered considerable losses, particularly from Allied aviation, and it required all the troops of their tactical reserve to maintain the various and complicated positions along the lines now existing. But they were holding, and an important difficulty had begun to develop on our side, where the casualties had been far above expectations and the flow of replacements far below. The difficulty arose in part from the failure of the Selective Service System to meet the army's requirements in manpower; in part, from the army itself, which had over-manned such formations as air force ground crews, military police, supply corps and headquarters paper-work units, while undersupplying the combat infantry to a precisely equal extent.

THE next attempt to break through the Cassino position came in March, 1944, and was an effort to make use of the growing Allied superiority in the air. The ancient monastery on the hill had thus far been spared because of its religious significance, but as Allied forces inched forward on both sides it became clear that the building was the key of the whole position. It was therefore announced that it would be bombed. On March 22, Allied planes working in relays gave the place the heaviest bombardment any spot of similar size had ever received. The monastery was reduced to rubble and the ground around it torn to pieces, but when our infantry came forward toward evening they found so many Germans holding out in the ruins that the attack could not be pressed home. The bombing, like the days of drumfire to which Western front positions were subjected in 1916, had only succeeded in tearing up the ground so that neither supplies nor artillery could be brought forward.

After this failure, there was a long period of quiescence, during which the Fifth and Eighth armies were regrouped and new troops brought in, while the air forces hammered unremittingly at German communications and produced a gradual weakening in ways that were not at once apparent. The Anzio beachhead was gradually reinforced till it contained three American and two British infantry divisions, an American armored division, and various special groups amounting to another division in strength, the whole under the command of Major General Lucian K. Truscott. Two fresh American divisions were placed on the Appian Way front of the Garigliano line; the British Eighth Army, reinforced by Polish troops, took over the whole sector from the Adriatic to below Cassino.

The new plan was for the Eighth Army to sweep round the lofty summit of Mt. Tyro behind Cassino and get down into the upper reaches of the Liri valley, while the Fifth attacked by its left along the shore with naval help, and Truscott's men broke out of their beachhead. The German forces were now commanded by Marshal Von Kesselring; they had some twelve divisions in line on the southern front with five more surrounding the Anzio beachhead and another eight in army reserve. But most of these divisions were under strength, so the Allies possessed somewhat the superior forces. Moreover, Allied air superiority had become overpowering, and in Italy, at least, transportation had been recognized as the major German weakness. Our planes had bombed out every railroad yard and nearly every bridge below

Florence before the attack opened on May 11 all along the line.

Truscott delayed for a brief time to induce the Germans to send as many men as possible to their southern front. Among the hills the French and British got through, and on May 16 Cassino fell with 1,500 prisoners, while along the coast the green American division made steady if somewhat slow progress. By the 20th the Eighth Army was making good advances up the main road through Cassino and it became apparent that the Germans were withdrawing—it was supposed to another system of defenses called "The Hitler Line," which had been much spoken of.

On the 23rd General Truscott launched his attack—the British elements driving straight toward Rome, while the American attacked northeast towards Cisterna on the Appian Way, which had been the objective point of the beachhead fighting. Von Kesselring had pulled his artillery back in anticipation of such a move and made an extremely good defense, holding tightly to the key communication centers on the two main roads—Velletri and Valmontane—until he extricated the bulk of his formations. The chief gains along the ground were thus merely territorial, but this warfare of movement forced the Nazis to use the roads even by daylight; they lost heavily to the Allied air forces in the process and were now unable to find a stabilizing position in the Alban hills anywhere south of Rome. On June 2 the Velletri-Valmontane line was broken when infantry scaled the summit between the two towns, and on June 4 Allied columns were marching into Rome.

From this point the roads fan out in several directions. The pursuers followed close on the Germans, who were in some disorder, and the prospect of following still more vigorously to convert the retreat into a rout must have been an attractive one. But over-all strategic considerations intervened. When Rome fell, the scheduled invasion of northern France was only twenty-four hours away and it was essential to prepare for the support of this operation by an attack through southern France with a reconstituted Seventh Army and French forces. In mid-June three American and four French divisions were taken out of line to prepare for this operation, being replaced by fewer and less-experienced troops.

Moreover, our men were now advancing through the country where roads and bridges had been devastated by our air forces, to which the Germans had added by demolitions carried out with their usual skill, so that as the lines lengthened supply became a serious problem. The drive slowed. In mid-July the Germans made a stout defense before the important port of Leghorn, which had to be taken by an encirclement from the east after a preliminary operation had gained heights for artillery support. By the end of that same month the Germans were back to the Arno River, which is deep and wide; the heights on its north bank afforded them the artillery observation posts they knew so well how to use. Here the position stabilized.

THE submarine war had really been won in 1943; Admiral King issued a statement in March of 1944 which honestly said that these raiders had been changed from menace to problem. By this time the new types of torpedoes had been thoroughly mastered; destroyer escorts and escort carriers were appearing in such numbers that it was possible to give every convoy the opulent cover that had hitherto been provided only for a few of great importance. There was no longer any real hindrance in the flow of troops and supplies to Europe, a fact which aided immeasurably in planning the land operations there.

Moreover, the German order for submarines to fight matters out with planes had by this time brought unmitigated disaster upon the U-boat service. The plane-borne depth charge had been improved to a point where it was very deadly, and, given an aviator's ability to see a submarine some distance under the surface, the step of ordering them to fight planes might seem necessary. But once on the surface the submarine had no weapons that could cope with the gunpower of destroyers and destroyer escorts, which now invariably appeared soon after a plane had made contact.

The losses in these hopeless battles against the combined Allied forces almost invariably fell on the ablest and boldest submarine captains, those who most fully carried out the orders to stand and fight. The result was a perceptible break in the morale of the whole service at some time in 1944. Careful Nazi indoctrination prevented it from becoming a mutiny as a similar break had been in the previous war; but it was remarked that the U-boats had lost the spirit of the offensive. They waited for the opportunities provided by a crippled ship or a badly maneuvering convoy, returned from cruises with full loads of torpedoes, or fired them off uselessly and reported sinkings they had not made. In 1942 the German announcements of Allied tonnage sunk, compiled from submarine commanders' reports, had been within measurable distance of the facts, but in the middle of 1943 there began to be a considerable divergence, and by the end of another year, facts and German figures no longer bore any relation to each other.

The progress of a form of war in which individual battles were only incidents is perhaps best indicated statistically. In 1942 the Germans had lost 65 submarines, in return for which they sank 8,240,000 tons of shipping, or 97,059 tons for every submarine lost. In 1943, 237 submarines went down, but got only 3,611,000 tons of ships, 15,198 tons for each submarine. By 1944 the figures were 241 submarines sunk and only 1,422,000 tons of shipping, an average of 5,900 tons per U-boat lost. In the last year the majority of the ships plying the ocean were well over 5,900 tons in size, which means that Germany was paying more than one submarine for every ship sunk. At this rate the U-boat war was not an asset but a military liability.

Not so with the American submarine war against Japan. After the first burst of energy during the Singapore-Java campaign, when Allied underwater craft could operate from bases near at hand against large military convoys, there had been a falling off. The American submarine service was not a large one at the time. The boats, based on Australia, Midway, or the Aleutians, had long distances to go and many of them were required to abstain from offensive operations to conduct necessary scouting against the movements of the Japanese fleet. In mid-1943 the Japanese also introduced a new type of depth charge which caused us some losses.

But these losses were counted in ones and twos instead of the tens and twenties of the Germans, and by that time the American submarines had already made such serious inroads on the Japanese merchant marine that its gains since the beginning of the war by new construction and capture were entirely canceled. At least three factors contributed to this success. Vast though the Pacific is, the productive areas from which Japanese shipping operated were relatively few in number; currents and chains of reefs made the possible steaming routes still more limited—there was no such variety of choice possible as in the open Atlantic. Secondly, the Japanese proved inefficient antisubmarine men, few of them having the technical skills' necessary for the construction and operation of such devices as radar and supersonic gear, to which they added the psychologically bad quality of tending to fall into a panic or a temper at moments of stress.

The third and probably the determining cause lay within the American submarine service itself, an organization composed entirely of volunteers, who were admitted only after the most searching physical and mental examinations. Even under the pressure of war, no short-cuts in their training were permitted and great attention was given both to the comfort of the men while aboard and to adequate recreation while ashore after the long cruises —a sharp variation from the German practice. American submarines were also much helped by the improved radar and sound gear that began to appear in our boats, and late in 1943 by a new torpedo of great explosive power. As submarines poured from the yards (193 were commissioned in 1942–1944, a figure small beside the German but in total tonnage not so much less, since American submarines were nearly twice as large as theirs), their depredations became so serious as to affect the whole of Japanese strategy and economy.

The figures are somewhat approximate, since many Japanese ships were lost to mines and various combinations of submarines with other vessels, but as nearly as they can be determined they show that in 1943 American submarines sank 284 Japanese ships of 1,342,000 tons; in 1944, 492 ships of 2,388,000 tons, or nearly double the Allied shipping sunk by German submarines in the latter year. This far exceeded the Japanese replacement capacity and caused their national food rations, already at a subsistence level, to be reduced nearly a quarter. In the summer of 1944 a shortage of gasoline for even the most essential military purposes began to develop, since all Japanese oil had to come from the conquered lands to the south. Their program of general navy construction had already been constricted to provide more carriers; now many of the remaining ships were canceled in order to find steel for destroyers and other escort craft.

Even this proved insufficient. American submarines attacked not only the Japanese convoys but also their escorts, with great success. Down to the middle of 1944, American submarines had sunk some thirty Japanese destroyers, four light cruisers and one heavy, and two of the four escort carriers

Japan had managed to place in operation. Later the remaining escort carriers were sunk, with four large fleet carriers and a battleship. Submarines accounted for a total of 1,944 merchant craft, two thirds of all Japan had.

It was the operations of the submarines quite as much as anything that led to one of the most curious campaigns of the war. When the Japanese conquered Burma early in 1942 and brought their frontier up to the Assam Mountains that separate that country from India, they effectively isolated China from the Western Allies. China had no oil within her borders nor a munitions industry capable of producing anything beyond small arms. She had already been fighting for years and her armies had been reduced to something like guerrillas. Her collapse would place such vast resources in the hands of the Japanese that it was considered essential to do something for her. The problem was not so much strictly a military one as one of engineering.

General Joseph H. Stilwell, "Vinegar Joe," a forthright, energetic, and unconventional soldier, had been sent to eastern India at the outbreak of the war and had participated in the retreat from Burma. Major-General Claire Chennault, who had recruited a group of American fliers for service with the Chinese on a mercenary basis before Pearl

Harbor, was commissioned into the American air force. The first operation was to set up an aerial ferry over "the hump" of the Himalayas for absolutely essential materials. The second was to establish the 14th Air Force under General Chennault's command, operating from bases in South China. This force gave some support to China and greatly harassed the Japanese, though the amount of material damage done was small because of the difficulty of flying supplies in. At the same time the returning ferry planes brought out a number of Chinese soldiers who were trained under Stilwell's command with American arms and weapons. These men, in conjunction with the British Indian Army and a minute American expeditionary force, succeeded in 1943 in winning back part of northern Burma. Across this area, American engineers and Chinese labor began constructing a road with a parallel pipeline right through the heart of the mountains, one of the most gigantic engineering projects ever undertaken. The road ("Ledo Road," later "Stilwell Road") was not finished till late in 1944, but the Air Transport Command increased rapidly in efficiency and by June of that year was able to support another project.

This was the bombardment of the Japanese homeland and the steel factories in Manchuria. After difficulties and many delays American engineers had at last succeeded in constructing a

monster plane capable of flying the Atlantic and
back with a bomb load. As fast as these B-29s
came into production they were shipped to the
East, and at the bases in South China a formation
was built up. On June 15, 1944, the bombers took
off for the first time on a combat mission, flying
to the great steel mills at Yawata in southern Japan. They bombed the mills and made the return
journey without loss. Repeated raids followed; the
new machine had a revolutionary fire-control system, and Japanese fighters found themselves unable to cope with the big bombers.

The reaction of the enemy was immediate and
somewhat unexpected. Instead of seeking new
means for dealing with the big planes in the air,
they opened an offensive along the ground in southern China designed to cut the bases from under
them. Since the beginning of the American war
the Japanese had treated China more as a training
area than as an actual theater, sending the new
conscripts thither for a campaign which gained a
few miles each year but accomplished little for the
old imperial ambition of setting up a rail-and-road
line from the productive areas in the south to ports
at Shanghai and in Korea from which it would be
a short voyage, through easily protected waters, to
Japan.

The depredations of American submarines had
now made such a road imperative if the Japanese

wished to keep their war machine going. The attacks of the B-29s merely furnished an additional reason. The Japanese threw heavy forces into the area and, in a confused campaign that washed up to the borders of the province of which Chungking is the center, won all the American air bases by the end of the summer.

CHAPTER XII

THE IMPERIAL DEFENSE-LINE COLLAPSES

By the late spring of 1944 the outer protective
screen of the Japanese empire had been thrown
down. The capture of Kwajalein and Eniwetok in
the Central Pacific and the steady advance of General MacArthur's forces along the shores of New
Guinea in the south had isolated among the islands
so many of the enemy's best troops that the make-
up of his army was seriously affected. His great
bases at Truk and Rabaul were converted into useless appendages which would only become func-
tional again if he regained control of the sea. Even
so, it was impossible for the Allies to drive home
an attack against either Japan or the stolen Indies.
Beginning with Japan itself, a great semicircle of
islands sweeps down below the equator, each within
easy flying distance of the next, all strongly fortified
and provided with fields for the planes on which
the Japanese were now placing great reliance.

From this protective chain the heart of the empire was distant by a mileage almost equal to the

width of the Atlantic. Some point in this circle must be seized and set up as an American base before the true attack could begin. The most centrally located and therefore the most strategically desirable of these island points were those of the Marianas group—Guam, Saipan, and Tinian—whose seizure would cut the main line of enemy communications southward and whose possession would furnish new fields for the B-29s, in addition to the advantages they had as harbors. As soon as Eniwetok had been secured, therefore, and reserves of material accumulated, it was decided to strike for the Marianas, a strategic concept which seems to owe much to the bold mind and long-range view of Fleet Admiral Ernest King.

The over-all commander for the Marianas operation was Admiral Raymond Spruance. His Fifth Fleet was divided into the fast carrier task force of Vice-Admiral Marc A. Mitscher and the battleship force of Vice-Admiral Lee. They were to furnish preliminary bombardments and cover against any operations of the Japanese navy, which was expected to emerge from its retirement for the defense of so vital an area. Close support of the landings was to be provided by a squadron of old battleships under Rear-Admiral J. L. Oldendorf and by groups of escort carriers, here used for the first time in major combat operations. The landing force was two divisions of Marines and one of army

The Marianas

PACIFIC

OCEAN

troops (27th), all under command of Marine Major-General Holland Smith.

The attack was set for middle June and a number of subsidiary operations were undertaken to conceal to the last moment the precise point of impact—bombing raids by B-24s from the Aleutians, the first attacks of the B-29s on the Japanese homeland, and a series of long-range raids from bases in the MacArthur area against such points as Truk and Palau in the Carolines. The initial landing was to be made on Saipan. The general plan was for Mitscher's fast carriers to fly strikes from some distance out on June 12 to destroy the local Japanese air defenses and to begin the attack against defenses aground. The fast battleships would follow with a gunnery attack. It was expected that the first Japanese reaction would be to stage down quantities of relief air groups through the Bonins. Mitscher would divide his forces after the first attack, sending two of his fast carrier groups north to strike at the Japanese among these islands. Meanwhile the escort carriers and slow battleships would arrive off Saipan with the landing forces, and these more deliberate units would provide support and cover for the invasion, while Mitscher's carriers and Lee's battleships were left free to deal with any move by the Japanese fleet.

The enemy scout planes managed to work through Mitscher's patrols and caught sight of his armada a day early. As a result he speeded up his attack, striking the Marianas fields on June 11 instead of the 12th and repeating the attack the following day with gunnery help from the battleships. By afternoon of this second day the local Japanese air groups in the Marianas had been disposed of with little loss to ourselves. On the 13th the escort carriers arrived with Oldendorf's battleships and Vice-Admiral J. J. Clark was detached for the run up to the Bonins. He arrived on the 15th in weather so heavy there was some doubt whether planes could be flown at all. Nevertheless his strike groups got away and achieved surprise on the Japanese at Chichi Jima, Haha Jima, and Iwo Jima, where, exactly as expected, planes in considerable numbers were discovered on their way down to the Marianas and were very nearly wiped out in a two-day strike.

The Marines had meanwhile been flung on the beaches at the southwestern face of Saipan on both sides of the sugar-mill town of Charan Kanoa. The preliminary shelling and bombing was far heavier than at Kwajalein or Eniwetok, but Saipan is a large steep island of igneous rock. As soon as the advance to the beach began, it became clear that the Japanese had many guns still in action among the rocks and ravines.

Casualties at the southern of the two landing points were high, the concealed enemy guns firing with great accuracy at a line of reef and smashing

up both most of the amphibious tanks and the landing vessels loaded with artillery. The objective for
the day was not reached, but the two landings
joined up and when at daybreak of the second day
the Japanese tried a tank attack at the center it
was completely broken up by fire from the ships.
The Japanese began to retire to the steep slopes of
Mt. Tapotchau which furnishes the central backbone of the island, as the Marine force pivoted
on its left to drive them in that direction. But the
enemy had both greater forces and better positions
than anticipated. It was necessary to put in the
army division, which it had been hoped to hold
in reserve for the scheduled operation against
Guam. These troops were moved in behind the
Marines at the southern beachhead and thrust eastward toward the island's big airfield, Aslito. It was
slow work as the Japanese had many ingenious positions in caves with armored doors which opened
just long enough to let concealed guns fire. But by
the 19th the army men had gained control of the
airfield.

NOT since October, 1942, had the Japanese carrier
forces been in action. In the interval since that
time their naval air service had been completely
reconstructed—new pilots trained, new carriers in
service. Now in June, 1944, they had available five
large carriers (three of them larger than any of

ours) and four of the lighter type. The staff had
worked out an ingenious plan for their employment
in the defense of the Marianas. Powerful air
groups, at least equal to the strength of three or
four carriers more, would be staged down through
the Bonins to fall on our ships, which must neces-
sarily stay near the landing points to furnish cover
for the troops. At the same time the enemy fleet
would leave its haunts in the Carolines and Philippines, run north to a point in the Philippine Sea
about 700 miles from the Marianas, and there fly
off its planes. Seven hundred miles is double the
range of a carrier plane and the Japanese carriers
would turn away as soon as these planes were
launched, thus preventing any counterattack by
the American carrier aircraft which had dealt so
severely with them before. But the Japanese dive
bombers and torpedo planes would inevitably find
our fleet so close to the Marianas that, after having
struck our ships a blow, the planes could land there
and then repeat the attack from fields in the
islands.

One part of this plan miscarried when Admiral
Spruance anticipated it and sent Clark's carriers
north to break up the Japanese air groups among
the Bonins. But in exchange for this the enemy
had a most encouraging report from its commander
on Saipan, Admiral Nagumo, that he had sunk
at least one American battleship, damaged several

carriers and other vessels, and that the beachhead was only weakly held. Part of this was the result of a fake landing attempt meant to be "repulsed"; the rest can be accounted for only by the Japanese system of politeness, which did not allow commanders to report to the Emperor anything less than success.

The Japanese had, however, suffered another disaster of which they were still ignorant. As their fleets made north to the Carolines they had been spotted by American submarines as early as the 14th and had been reported to Admiral Spruance. The submarines continued to trail them. As the Japanese planes flew off on the morning of June 19, the submarine *Cavalla* closed in and put three torpedoes into the veteran large carrier *Shokaku,* and *Albacore* hit the new carrier *Taiho* with another torpedo. Far to the east that same morning the army troops had captured Aslito field. Admiral Spruance turned southwest, with his battleships between the carriers and the onrushing Japanese, and cleared his decks by sending all the dive bombers in to tear up Orote Point Field on Guam, the last one in the Marianas where enemy planes could land. His fighter patrols were all up, so numerous that they alone outnumbered all the machines that the Japanese had in the air. They encountered their enemies while the latter were still in cruising formation and at cruising level.

The Japanese attack thus became a complete failure; they secured but one bomb hit, on the armor of a battleship where it did little damage. Four hundred and two Japanese planes were shot down for the greatest loss to an air service of any single day in the war, and even the planes that escaped crashed on landing. The Japanese naval air service, so carefully rebuilt, had been destroyed with a single blow.

Admiral Spruance hung in the offing until nearly twilight, uncertain whether there might not be more Japanese planes behind these. When it developed that there were not, he speeded up on the trail of the enemy fleet, now making for the shelter of the Ryukyus. The next day, June 20, he pursued all day, confident that he could overtake them if they were following their usual practice of trying to get the damaged carrier home. Late in the afternoon they were found at the very limit of airplane range from our carriers, and though, if sent out, strike groups could not return to our ships till after dark, Spruance flew them off.

They reached the Japanese fleet about 6:00 P.M. in fading light and found it well scattered, with almost no fighter protection and running fast. Our own planes had also became somewhat scattered during the search and the attack lacked the coördination of some that had been delivered earlier in the war, but it was deadly enough. All the big

Japanese carriers were hit and two of the light ones
—one of the latter so heavily that although she
was dragged home she never again put to sea.
Shokaku had gone down as a result of the submarine *Cavalla's* torpedoes; the *Taiho,* largest carrier in the enemy service, had blown up; the big
Hitaka sank as the result of air attacks and her
sister *Hayataka* was taken home in such condition
that she too was out of the war. A destroyer was
sunk and two of the fast tankers upon which the
Japanese fleet depended for long-range mobility.

Our forces paid for their victory with 47 planes,
mostly lost in crash or water landings in the dark
when they had returned to their carriers with their
last drops of fuel. Many of the aviators were saved
when Admiral Mitscher, though deep in enemy
waters, took the bold step of flinging the fleet's
searchlight beams aloft as homing beacons.

WHILE the American fleet was taking in its planes
far to the west on that evening of June 20, 1944,
a minor air attack had come upon the ships grouped
off Saipan and smashed one of them. The planes
could clearly have come from nowhere but down
the line of the Bonins, and to Admirals Spruance
and Mitscher it seemed that this might be the
beginning of a new effort in force. Admiral Clark
with his carrier groups was rushed back to Iwo
Jima. The diagnosis proved correct; he found the

place swarming with Japanese planes and fought a severe air battle with them on the 22nd. Like some of the formations encountered among the Solomons, these Japanese seemed to have been poorly or hastily trained. They lost 60 planes against only two of ours, and, after more of them had been destroyed on the ground in a second attack, the remainder turned back to Japan.

On shore the 4th Marine Division had worked right across the island to its eastern beaches and had turned north. The army division, leaving some formations behind to clear out the caves, moved into the center of the line around Mt. Tapotchau. They were slow in the movement and slow in attacking after it. The Japanese managed to reorganize around their central position and push infiltration attacks into the flanks of the two Marine divisions. Because of this, a famous controversy later developed: army leaders claimed that their more deliberate method of procedure saved lives; the Marines insisted that their rapid smashing attacks broke the back of resistance early and made mopping up largely a matter of careful patrolling. The question is technical; but there seems to have been something wrong with the leadership of the army division, which made its attacks with poor coördination throughout. Finally, after the advance had worked slowly forward, against the type of opposition always given by the Japanese, till it reached a point four miles from the tip of the island, the enemy counterattacked.

It was a suicide charge, which might have been expected, but it broke through the 27th, wiping out one of its battalions, and got in among the Marine artillery positions. Many of the 15,000 casualties in the land fighting on Saipan occurred on this occasion, and the commander of the army division was removed. The Japanese dead on the island numbered over 28,000; many more were sealed in caves, never to be counted, some of them not being disposed of till six months after July 10, when the conquest of the island was declared complete.

The necessity of beating off the Japanese fleet and the prolonged resistance on Saipan had thrown the attack on Guam out of schedule, as also that against the small island of Tinian, which is within artillery range of southern Saipan. The double task was undertaken on July 21, that is, as soon as new troop formations could be staged from the United States and Hawaii through the Marshalls. The 3rd Marine Division, a Marine provisional brigade almost a division strong, and the 77th Army Division were involved.

There was no Japanese opposition by sea this time and the enemy air forces had been driven off, so the harassments and distractions were far less. Nevertheless the campaign itself showed that the lessons of Saipan had been well learned. Ships and planes kept up such close and constant support that organized resistance was broken by August 10, without any formal battles. Seven thousand of the 17,000 Japanese killed on the island were not eliminated till after this date. The fanaticism of the resistance is indicated by the fact that the prisoners numbered only 483.

As soon as the islands were secured, great numbers of both army and navy construction workers were moved in, the latter to set up naval base installations for the move forward against the heart of the Japanese empire, the former to provide the long landing fields and elaborate shop installations necessary to support a large force of B-29 bombers. The battles in the Marianas had given us the gateway to Japan and a centralized assembly point from which any place around the great circuit of the empire could be attacked. They had also resulted in the virtual destruction of the most powerful arm of the Japanese fleet—though this was not realized at the time, since it was not known how heavy the damage had been to the enemy carriers in the great action of June 19–20, a victory fully as decisive as Midway.

CHAPTER XIII

THE GREAT INVASION

THE assault on what Hitler called "The Fortress of Europe" was primarily a logistic operation, a question of getting adequate supplies ashore to enable our troops to maintain themselves once they had landed, and of keeping up from the rear a flow of food, ammunition, and equipment. The Germans had systematically stripped the districts along the coast; the experience of Italy showed that their destruction of everything that would serve an army was so thorough that the attacking forces might almost as well be pitched into a jungle. Until the supply problem was solved, tactical and strategic questions could not even be considered.

The Germans were known to have made the problem as difficult as possible by heavily fortifying and garrisoning all the ports along the coast of Europe with quay capacity sufficient to support an army. The ports themselves were heavily mined and had immense numbers of guns of all calibres so mounted as to bear both out to sea and inward toward the land approaches; smaller pieces sup-

plied interlocking belts of fire to cover the forts
from infantry infiltration. The artillery positions
were usually dug into hill slopes or heavily covered
with concrete as a protection against air attack;
many of the guns were those removed from the
Maginot Line.

Between the ports, at all the beaches where landings might reasonably be expected, an immense
amount of work had been done by laborers impressed from eastern Europe. Underwater obstacles, mainly of steel, had been deeply planted and
linked together to tear the bottoms out of landing
craft. Many beaches were mined in addition. In
general, the strands of France are backed at a little
distance by a line of bluffs; here artillery of all
calibres had been mounted, the foreshore and all
the open country behind the bluffs had been
studded with tank traps, and practically all the
small cottages so common in this part of France
had been evacuated of their inhabitants and converted into pillboxes. In all these installations
there were permanent garrison troops, under orders to know the country thoroughly.

The German system of defense, of course, had
the disadvantage of locking up many troops, some
of their best, in fortresses at the very perimeter of
the territory to be defended, and leaving the German area commanders weak in mobile reserves for
counterattacking once a landing had been effected.

It was a handicap they felt constrained to accept, not only because the Allied strength in aviation and vehicles made a war of movement peculiarly favorable to our side but also because the spring of 1944 brought American heavy bomber formations to Europe in such vastly increased numbers that 1,000-plane raids became common and there were some that doubled this figure.

The characteristic feature of the air war in the winter and spring of 1944 was a shift in emphasis on the part of the attack to the Luftwaffe, which was assailed both directly in the skies and at its fields, and indirectly at its factories. By May a diminution in the German fighter strength was encountered. This was not because there was a pronounced falling off in numbers of the German fighters but because of the comparative decrease in numbers through the enormous growth of the U.S. Eighth Air Force, which had by this time come to outnumber the home-based British. Bombing had not succeeded in wiping out German factories; by dispersing and digging in they managed to stay in production. But the damage caused was so serious—especially in places like the great railroad hub of Berlin, more than three quarters of which was burned out in a series of raids during March— that it was clear to the Nazi High Command that so formidable a force of bombers could make military movements around the area of a landing more than a little uncertain. This furnished them with an additional reason for basing their defense on clinging to the seaports, with delaying defense elsewhere and counterattack against the Allied means of communication.

This was known to be the German method and it dictated Allied strategy. Our forces must contemplate taking a major army into Europe across open beachheads and supporting them in the same manner perhaps throughout an entire campaign, for there was no guarantee that a port could be won at an early date or that it would be any more useful than Naples after it had been gained. In turn, this had much to do with the choice of the spot for the invasion. It had to be an area which the larger type of landing craft could reach directly from England without the necessity of loading and unloading from transports. It had to be one from which troops could operate under the constant protection of Allied air power until they had won ground enough to provide their own strips; it should be a place near a good harbor and where the German communications were subject to bombing attack.

These conditions were met by the Cotentin Peninsula of Normandy, and it was upon this peninsula that the choice fell—a major factor being that the German communications ran back across the deep and wide Seine River and that there were numerous bottlenecks at the bridges. Thinking we might strike there, the Germans deployed one army group with reserves and armor to meet the attack. But precisely because of the communications question they considered it quite as probable that the attack would come in the region of Calais, which was not only far nearer the English coast but had the added advantage that our advance could be made without supply lines stretching back across the Seine and Somme. The adjacent ports were also more numerous and better. The Germans accordingly deployed their second and larger army group in the Calais area.

For the solution of the fundamental problem of ports the Allies conceived the device of two completely artificial harbors, with breakwaters partly constructed of worn-out ships but mainly of huge caissons set up in England. The question of landing craft admitted of no solution through ingenuity; neither did that of supplies. The second, indeed, caused so much difficulty and involved so many executive decisions that for many months it occupied nearly all the time of General Eisenhower and his staff to the exclusion of more purely military problems. On more than one occasion the suggestion was made by those highest in governmental and military circles that the whole invasion plan be postponed or limited in scope.

Mr. Churchill in particular entered continual ob-

jections; he had always wished to invade Europe
from the south, and though at the historic Quebec
conference of May, 1943, his arguments had been
overborne and the decision taken, he always found
new questions to raise. Not the least of General
Eisenhower's titles to fame is that he insisted on
pushing "Operation Overlord" (as it was called)
through as planned and that he managed to see a
way through each objection from below and interference from political sources as these came up. He
insisted that the whole fate of the war depended
upon this invasion; that a failure or a partial success would return the initiative to the Germans as
their own failure in Egypt and partial success in
Russia had transferred it to the Allies. Again and
again officers of the highest rank and greatest
ability approached the General with suggestions
that the plan for aviation support would not work
—that the underwater obstacles would prove fatal
—that the invasion ought to be cut to three divisions in the initial stages—and particularly that the
plan of landing three airborne divisions would produce casualties up to 70 or 80 percent. To all he
replied, "I will take the responsibility," and insisted
that the plan of the Quebec conference be carried
through as made.

The question of landing craft, however, was one
he could not solve alone. They must be used in vast
numbers to make the initial wave of assault very

strong, so that the beachheads could be rapidly extended to a distance that would make it impossible for the Germans to interrupt the flow of supplies and reinforcements by gunfire. The Sicilian landing had succeeded rapidly because this was achieved; the landings at Salerno and Anzio had been strategic failures because it was not achieved. The shipyards, now relieved of some of the pressure for anti-submarine vessels, broke all records in supplying landing craft, but by March it was already evident that they could not meet the requirements for the invasion to begin in May, as originally planned. The date was shoved back to early June, though this placed it at the edge of a dangerous season for winds and tides. The invasion of south France, which was scheduled to take place simultaneously, was moved along to a time when the landing craft which had been used in Normandy could be shipped thither for the second invasion.

THE attack on the continent of Europe began tactically toward the middle of March, 1944, with a double change in tactics by the Allied bombers. The damaged Luftwaffe was still capable of mounting powerful local operations, and neither the bombing of factories nor the burning out of whole cities was bringing it down as rapidly as desired. On the other hand, the Mediterranean Air Force had badly damaged the Rumanian refineries and there was evidence that German ground transport on the long Russian front was beginning to suffer from a shortage of gasoline. Long-range bombers, both British and American, were concentrated against German synthetic oil plants, installations which it was impossible either to conceal or to place underground. Other targets were attacked, of course, but only as diversions or when, for some reason, a formation could not reach its primary objective.

At the same time the short-range bombers were fanned out all across northern France in a series of raids against communicaions, particularly railroads and bridges. These raids were on the whole very effective. By the date of the invasion the German transportation system in northern France was in such a state of disorganization that, if the area were not actually isolated, major military movements could only be made slowly. On the night of June 5 a thousand British heavy bombers suddenly attacked the whole Normandy coast. At daybreak the task was taken over by as many American planes, and under lowering skies of the following dawn the invasion was launched.

To furnish gunnery cover, six battleships stood in offshore, accompanied by a host of lighter vessels both British and American. A good many of the latter were lost, more from mines than from the shore batteries with which the German Commander, Rommel, hoped to make the invasion a

failure while it was still on the water. The general
Allied plan of operation was designed to break
down precisely such a defense, with both ships and
planes assigned in great numbers to attack targets
on call from troop leaders at the beach. Four thousand boats of various sizes were employed in the
landing; not even from a plane could all be seen
at once, so far did the armada stretch across the
horizon.

The tactical plan called for the British Second
Army (Montgomery) to land at the mouth of the
Orne River, advance as quickly as possible to the
line Bayeux-Caen, and there form a fighting defensive flank. An airborne division preceded them
to the region of Caen, and other airborne troops
were dropped as far away as Havre and Rouen to
interrupt enemy communications and to conceal
the true point of the main effort.

The beach landing in this area was successful
against comparatively light opposition and the airborne men gained possession of bridges across the
Orne north of Caen, but the aerial effort south of
that town failed, and during the four days following the invasion Rommel put an armored division
through Caen which drove the British from their
partial possession of the town and from most of
the Orne bridges. But at the same time the Second
joined its beachheads, captured Bayeux, and over-
ran an area seven miles deep, while Rommel's ar-

The Cotentin Peninsula

Prepared by Robert W. Galvin expressly for WAR FOR THE WORLD

mored attack was broken up by guns from the sea.

Further west the main effort was made by American troops under the command of General Bradley, along a front aggregating some thirty miles, the over-all design being to break through across the Cotentin Peninsula and to isolate the port of Cherbourg for attack from the rear. As soon as Cherbourg fell, major forces were to be poured in for a drive into Brittany. Two airborne divisions preceded the landing to gain communication points. There were two beachheads; Utah Beach on the west and Omaha Beach. At Utah Beach, Major General Collins's VII Corps broke through light resistance early, crossed a belt of marshes, and hooked up with the 82nd Airborne Division to capture the important road junction of Carentan, half cutting German communications with Cherbourg. This was accomplished by June 10.

The most difficult situation was encountered by Major General Gerow's V Corps (1st and 29th Divisions) at Omaha Beach, between Utah Beach and the British landing. The mines and underwater obstacles had not been effectively cleared either by demolition squads or fire. They wrecked many of the landing craft, and the advance elements of engineer troops found themselves so pinned down by fire that they could not accomplish their task of breaching the barbed wire and the system of antivehicle obstacles. The fire came from guns mounted in a series of low sandy bluffs that looked down onto the beach from a few hundred yards back. There was so much earth and concrete over these guns that they were immune to air attack and they were so well armored as to be impervious to destroyer fire. The battleships had to be summoned with their powerful artillery and while they were firing, elements of the 1st and 29th were heavily counterattacked by a German infantry division which, by the purest chance, had been conducting anti-invasion maneuvers at just this point.

Throughout June 6 and most of the 7th the struggle at Omaha Beach was close and doubtful and the casualties heavy, but the 2nd Division poured through the remnants of the two leaders and, attacking southwest, won a communication point which isolated the German front line. The Germans were holding in natural positions formed by hedgerows of ancient growth, so tangled and with ditches so deep as to halt tanks, but their defense was parceled out and local because of the difficulty of moving troops. The counterattack by air failed completely.

By June 12 the beachhead lines were growing; enough dry ground had been won near Carentan for the Allies to begin setting up landing strips. The British were twenty miles in, we had 16 divisions on the shore, and the VII Corps had established a mass of maneuver on its own right flank. American casualties in getting the beachheads established were slightly over 7,300.

In the second phase of the invasion the British attacked Caen while General Collins's mass of maneuver, headed by the 82nd and the veteran 9th Division, struck straight across the Cotentin Peninsula, reaching the west coast on June 18. Thanks to the pinning effect of the British attack and their own troubles in moving troops, the Germans had now lost communication with Cherbourg. But on that same day, the 18th, came a check when one of the worst gales in the whole history of the English Channel blew up; it was to last four days.

The work of putting the artificial ports in position had begun as soon as our forces pushed far enough inland to eliminate the danger of German artillery, and it was now in full swing. The storm completely wrecked the port behind the American area at Omaha Beach, piling the shore so high with debris that engineering equipment destined for the front had to be diverted to the task of merely making a clearing. The British port at Arromanches was severely damaged and the caissons salvaged from Omaha had to be used to repair it. Instead of two artificial ports the invasion was now supported by only one, and that one long delayed. The shortage of equipment was felt at once, particularly in such items as tanks and shop equipment, not very susceptible of being brought in across open beaches.

Moreover, the lowering skies of the storm almost completely blacked out the Allied infantry coöperation plans. Now for various reasons our command had decided to use planes for counterbattery work, long-range fire, and for other missions usually assigned to heavy artillery. Our troops were thus suddenly without this form of support while the Germans did have heavy artillery and their service was already superior in light pieces and mortars. The result was that for the time being they had fire superiority. Allied armor could hardly move; repeated infantry attacks by the British failed, and the south face of the front across the Cotentin Peninsula stabilized in a type of warfare resembling that of World War I.

On the northern front toward Cherbourg, German strength had been badly broken in the rush across the peninsula, and when General Collins put three divisions into the attack the enemy retreated to the area of his fortified port. By June 22 the siege began. The place was protected on the landward side by a series of hills, the whole interiors of which had been dug out and heavy guns mounted on several stories. These positions had to be assaulted by infantry advancing inch by inch under cover of constant shelling and bombing. A thousand heavy bombers were used in the attack on the 22nd. The battleships lay off the port, firing almost continuously; and one of them, *Texas*, suffered considerable damage from German guns.

The enemy's defense was conducted with great tactical skill. At night they counterattacked constantly, and once they won back a big fort that had already been captured. But as Allied control of the air was absolute, the Americans were able to move at will, concentrating now in one direction, now another. After a week of savage street fighting Cherbourg fell on June 27. Demolitions had been so thorough, and the harbor had been so completely blocked by mines, concrete, and sunken ships, that it was August before the first cargoes could come through. American casualties had now run to 23,000; but in Cherbourg the German loss had been nearly that number in prisoners alone.

THE British meanwhile had again and again attacked in the Caen region, a slow, dull, dogged fight under heavy artillery barrages which gained a few feet a day. On July 9 they had most of the town. After Cherbourg fell, the full American force swung into line with them, two fresh corps were landed to complete the American First Army, and the same type of advance began all across the peninsula. There were no tactics except at the lowest level; it was a straight slugging advance whose objective was to gain room for the employment of our troops. Every field with its hedgerows was a separate fortress and had to be reduced by siege operations, very costly in lives.

But the Germans were so harried by our aviation behind the lines and their reserves were so ground down by the ceaseless pressure of the British that they could not assemble forces for any major counterattack. They were forced to use their armor in support of small piecemeal attacks of about a battalion strength aimed at blunting the point of each successive Allied penetration. Early in July the hedgerow defenses lost much of their validity when American forces began mounting bulldozer scoops on the front of heavily armored tanks and driving them right through. Their air forces gave the Germans no help; thanks to their transportation troubles, they were constantly embarrassed for lack of gasoline and sometimes of ammunition. Toward the end of June they lost Marshal Rommel, their Supreme Commander, when he was mortally wounded by a bullet from an Allied plane that caught him on the road in his car.

His replacement was Marshal Rundstedt, one of the ablest of the German commanders, who had played a great part in the drive through France in 1940. Before he could develop a new strategy of his own, General Bradley's men, after two weeks of close and bloody fighting, captured the great road and railroad center of St. Lô, hub of the whole peninsula. Rundstedt reported to Berlin that his situation had become dangerous. His reserves, especially in armor, were almost exhausted. He could get no reinforcements from the rear and was not being allowed to draw on the unemployed German army in the Calais area, since the German High Command knew that we still had forces in England and expected us to attempt the Calais region with another landing. Rundstedt's suggestion was that he retreat from the Normandy region and all central France, building up a new line of defense behind the Seine. He believed he could hold this position, with the aid of the Calais troops.

The fact that so able a German commander could report in favor of abandoning the campaign is the best indication of the success of the only invasion of the European Continent ever achieved from the sea. To people on the Allied side it seemed that the gains were small and achieved at great cost, and this was true if geography alone were considered. But the whole structure of the German defense had been shaken. The army was so short of reserves that Polish and Russian prisoners were pressed into service.

Rundstedt's report fell in the period that witnessed an officers' conspiracy against the life of Adolf Hitler. The German Führer considered the report treasonable, ordered the position to be held at any cost, and removed Rundstedt. Thus at a critical juncture the enemy were driven to the discontinuity of strategy and method that follows such rapid changes in command, and the incoming leaders were forced to undertake a task they did not believe they could perform.

THE invasion had not taken place a moment too soon. On June 15, after the beachheads had been linked, observers in London saw a streak of flame down the sky and heard a heavy explosion. It looked like the crash of a German bomber and they cheered; but as three, four, and many others followed, they realized it could not be that and the cheering stopped. It was, in fact, the beginning of a new age in warfare.

The objects that had trailed across the sky were aerial torpedoes, each carrying about the same explosive charge as those used at sea and flying on a pair of short wings, pilotless, propelled by a jet or reaction motor which had a close affinity to the rocket. They had come from a series of carefully camouflaged ramps on the coast in the Calais area. Though their accuracy was low, the Germans had little difficulty in hitting a target so big as the city of London, against which most of the new weapons were aimed. Christened V-1 by the Germans and buzz-bombs by the Allies, the bombs flew very high and at a speed of over 400 miles an hour, so that only a very few fighter planes stood any chance of shooting them down. When their fuel was exhausted they nosed down at a sharp angle to explode.

The casualties they caused were considerable. By the end of July, 4,735 people had been killed in London and over 14,000 wounded. The material damage was far beyond that caused by the heaviest air raid—so serious was it, in fact, that in the opinion of many soldiers the invasion of France could not have been launched at all if the buzz-bomb attack had begun a few weeks earlier. Even as it was, it caused serious diversions of men and material from the attack on Europe. Barrage balloons around London were increased to over 2,000 in number. Over 1,350 anti-aircraft guns were brought down to the coast and established in batteries in an effort to catch the attacking robots before they could make their way inland. Many air squadrons and radar stations were told off to similar duties, while numerous planes were employed in bombing the launching sites.

They had been bombed before; in fact, the British had been aware that something of the sort was coming ever since the fall of 1943. In November of that year the Germans had already built over a hundred launching sites along the coast, every one of which was bombed out so that the work had to be begun again in the following spring. In fact,

the defense and counteroffense kept fairly well
ahead of the V-1 attacks. Of more than 8,000 of
the weapons launched only 2,300 reached their objective. Moreover, the Nazis spent so much time
and productive capacity on them that their air
service suffered severely. The attacks also had a
strategic effect unfavorable to the Germans by
helping to persuade them to detain in the Calais
area the troops that might have been much better
employed in Normandy.

CHAPTER XIV

FRANCE SET FREE

THE importance to an army of having a road-hub close behind its lines like that at St. Lô is that troops coming to it from a variety of directions may be fanned out along the radii of a circle, while the defenders must take the long way round the circumference. This was especially true in Normandy where the hedgerows and dense undergrowth made military traffic impossible except along the roads. When the American 29th Division captured St. Lô on July 18, 1944, after two weeks of desperate house-to-house fighting, and pushed the Germans two miles beyond, General Eisenhower was in a peculiarly good position for a major offensive against the left flank of the enemy line across the Cotentin Peninsula. That line swept in a curve around our front with its flank resting on the sea north of Coutances, and many of its supporting roads were under fire.

The strategic situation also was favorable. The German command had just changed for the second time within a month and some of the new staff officers were none too familiar with their duties. The violent attacks of the British Second Army and the Canadian First had unsettled their lateral communications at the root northeast of Caen. Reinforcements for the western end of the line had to go by a considerable circuit. To crown all, General George Patton, our best attack commander, had just landed through the beachhead ports with his Third Army, including no less than four armored divisions, a fact of which the Germans were still ignorant.

On July 25 General Eisenhower opened his offensive on a bright, sunny morning with a terrific bombardment from 1,575 heavy bombers, followed instantly by the same number of lighter planes. (An unfortunate feature of this attack was the death of Lieutenant General Lesley J. McNair, commander of the American ground forces, through an accidental bomb hit.) Great gaps were blasted in the hedgerows; through them poured four infantry divisions, headed toward Coutances on the coast against the opposition of only two German divisions. The bulk of the enemy strength was concentrated farther to the east against what they regarded as the very dangerous Canadian-British offensive. On the first day our troops gained two miles and cut one of the few lateral highways remaining to the enemy.

On the second day four entire divisions of tanks,

the first arrivals of the Third Army, rushed through the gap thus created. By July 28 the 4th Armored Division was in Coutances, from which point it turned southeast, hooking up with other armored formations and infantry to the east. The whole front now began to swing with St. Lô as a hinge. Many Germans were cut off and captured along the coast, as were many more in the area of the great break-through. Our forces found the enemy rear areas in a state of disorganization and captured whole companies that had not been able to obtain orders from their own headquarters. The First Army swung eastward against this door of the German left flank; the Third, General Patton in person up with the advance, fanned its 2nd, 3rd, 4th, and 6th Armored Divisions out to the coast at a dozen points.

On July 30 the 3rd Armored Division reached Avranches. This is an old walled town of 8,000 population, of considerable importance because its position at the head of a shallow estuary backed by rough country allows it to control access to all western Normandy. The few German troops in the place were able to hold it that day against the American vanguards, but by the next morning our infantry arrived and the town fell. That same day General Eisenhower reorganized his High Command, giving the First Army to Lieutenant General Courtney H. Hodges and making General

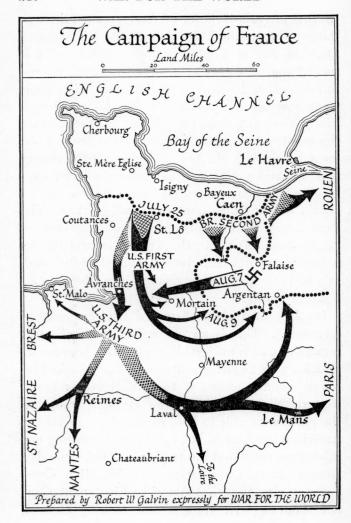

The Campaign of France

Land Miles

0   20   40   60

ENGLISH CHANNEL

Cherbourg

Bay of the Seine

Le Havre

Ste. Mère Eglise

Seine

ROUEN

Isigny

Bayeux

Caen

JULY 25

Coutances

St. Lô

BR. SECOND ARMY

U.S. FIRST ARMY

Falaise

Avranches

AUG. 7

St. Malo

Mortain

Argentan

BREST

U.S. THIRD ARMY

AUG. 9

ST. NAZAIRE

Mayenne

Reimes

Laval

PARIS

Le Mans

NANTES

Chateaubriant

To the Loire

Prepared by Robert W. Galvin expressly for WAR FOR THE WORLD

Bradley commander of an army group including both this force and General Patton's. Up to this time Montgomery had been theoretically in tactical charge of ground forces, though in a practical sense he had confined most of his attention to the British-Canadian portion of the front. His work in pinning down major German forces in that area had been excellent and had made possible the St. Lô break-through, but General Eisenhower was somewhat dissatisfied with his slowness in maneuver and, for the open-country operations now beginning, wished to draw on the enormous tactical skill and ability to make snap decisions of Omar Bradley, who had continually kept the Germans off balance on his front.

The Germans had withdrawn formations piecemeal in an attempt to save their crumbling left flank, where Hodges's attack threatened to roll up their whole line. Now, as the seriousness of the break-through fully justified Rundstedt's apprehensions and they realized that Patton was already in France, major forces were brought down from the Calais area. The six armored divisions that had been holding the position around Caen were shifted westward in a quick effort to break through the First Army's front toward Avranches. Fortunately for us, the German withdrawals weakened the Caen line before the troops from Calais could fill the gap. The Canadians and British attacked south-

ward and got across the lateral road to Avranches
on July 31. The result was that the German counterattack lacked both surprise and force. It made
some gains and for a time cut the corridor between
their left flank and the sea to some twelve miles.
But the American First Army held firm, and
through that 12-mile corridor General Patton continued to pour the Third Army in an endless stream
of tanks and truck-borne infantry.

By August 2 the 6th Armored was in Pontorson
and the 2nd Armored well along the Brittany coast
road at St. Malo. A compilation that day showed
that a week of continuous battles had given us
19,000 German prisoners; four more divisions of
enemy troops escaped only by rapid retreat into
Brittany. The very speed of the break-through,
indeed, militated against attaining one of the objectives in this direction. It had been hoped to
gain one of the great ports, Brest or Lorient, but
the Germans did not have time to move troops
out of these and when the armored columns of
Patton's men rolled up on August 7 they found
the enemy still strongly established in both places.

THE Breton ports had, however, become secondary
objectives by August 7, 1944, at which date the
entire province, except those ports, was cleared of
Germans and it was plain that General Hodges's
men would be able to hold the heavy and persistent

efforts to break through and cut off the Avranches corridor. By this date the dogged advance of the Canadians had broken through within only five miles of Falaise and a dazzling prospect opened up.

The bulk of the Nazi strength was now well to the north and west, between Vire and Mortain. Thanks to the operations of the Canadians the only highways the Germans had for supply or retreat ran in a southeasterly direction through Falaise and Argentan, thence back across the Seine as far east as Rouen and Paris. A large proportion of the Germans were slow foot-marching infantry with horse transport; and Patton was on the loose southward with strong formations of armor and mechanized infantry. If he could be swung north and east, major portions of that German army might be cut off; and while the effort would demand the utmost from men and machines, it was worth trying with such a driver as Patton behind it.

Bradley made another of his famous tactical snap decisions, and orders were issued to try the maneuver. Infantry and men of the French underground (*Maquis*) were sent to blockade the Breton ports, and the armor came streaming out of that province as rapidly as it had moved in. Other detachments ran south to hold the main bridges across the Loire against the rather unlikely possibility that the Germans in southern France would be able to organize a counterattack against Patton's new rear, as his main force hurried north with its weight on the right wing toward Le Mans. That town was assaulted on August 9 and taken from weak German formations; next day Alençon fell. Patton fanned mechanized troops out along the roads to Paris (they moved so rapidly that some had to be supplied by air) with directions to turn west toward Rouen, but the bulk of his strength was driven on Argentan.

The Canadians attacked south toward Falaise, the British east toward the mouth of the Seine. A special air force order called for every airplane fit for flight to be operated constantly against the Seine bridges and Germans in motion. The action, known as the battle of the Falaise Pocket, lasted until August 16. It was fought chiefly in rain, with the fiercest kind of fighting, day and night against Germans who had now fully realized their danger and who had planted extensive mine fields and brought up all the artillery they could muster to hold up the narrowing escape gap between Patton and the Canadians. Neither Argentan nor Falaise was taken during the battle and in a technical sense the German claim that their Seventh Army (the unit involved) escaped has some justification. But it was true only in the most restricted technical sense, for never was an army in worse condition than the German force whose remnants reached the north bank of the Seine on August 24.

They had lost 130,000 men in prisoners alone, a number exceeding all the Allied casualties put together since the invasion of France. Our forces buried 20,000 of their dead and if the wounded, who were never counted, reached the normal figure for fighting of this character, they were five to one of the killed. The German Seventh had lost nearly all its armor, most of its artillery and transport, and many of its headquarters staffs. It had in fact not so much escaped as been destroyed, and if toward the end of the month the port of Brest was able to beat off an assault it was chiefly because so many more of the enemy formations were now locked up in it and out of the war.

THE German unit occupying southern France was the Nineteenth Army, a formation well below the fighting-power level of those on the Atlantic coast. In that area, rougher and less populated than the industrial north, the French underground was particularly strong and had attained a considerable degree of military organization. The leadership was of the most varied sort; its activities ranged all the way from concealment of Allied aviators to attacks on means of communication and the assassination of collaborators with the Germans. It remained an essentially guerrilla organization, since the arms that were brought in by plane and submarine could consist of nothing beyond ma-

chine guns, grenades, and explosive charges, and
with these it was impossible to meet tanks or artillery. Yet the activity of the *Maquis* was greatly
intensified after Normandy was invaded; it soon
became so serious that more than half of the Nineteenth German Army was required merely to assure
communications for the rest. The result was that
the long southern coastline was held by only two
divisions and part of a third, while most of the
remaining Nineteenth Army formations were parceled out in small groups across the countryside,
in the worst possible position should the coast be
broken through.

The fact that the Allied landing was contemplated
was no secret from the Germans, whose aerial reconnaissance had spotted the ships of the invasion
fleet assembling in Corsican harbors. They de-
duced with approximate accuracy both the date
and the place of impact. But by this time
General Patton's whirlwind had already burst
through the German lines at Avranches in the
north; the German High Command was forced to
disregard appeals from the Nineteenth Army for
reinforcements and planes, and the attack fell upon
opponents struggling with a deep sense of dis-
couragement and insufficiency.

The blow was delivered by a new U.S. Seventh
Army under the command of Lieutenant-General
Alexander M. Patch (who had led the infantry on

Guadalcanal) and the First French Army of General De Lattre de Tassigny, the whole headed by Lieutenant-General Jacob L. Devers, who had shifted to the Mediterranean when Eisenhower returned to London. The point of impact was around Cannes and St. Raphael on the east face of the obtuse peninsula that juts into the Mediterranean between the mouths of the Rhone and the Italian border. The date was August 15, 1944; the battleships and cruisers that had covered the Normandy invasion were present for gunnery support with many French ships, and close-in air cover was provided by an assemblage of seven British and two American escort carriers, while heavy bombers came up from the fields of Corsica and Sardinia.

Before dawn on Invasion Day strong formations of parachutists descended in the valley of the Argens River, which reaches the sea at St. Raphael, to seize the pass by which the Rhone Valley is reached from the landing area. Other parachutists gained the pass by which the Germans might reinforce the area from north Italy, but the enemy attempted no such operation. Westward near Bornes in the great bay formed by the Hyères Islands, the French forces went ashore and with an armored division leading began pushing along the coast toward Toulon. On the eastern beaches the Americans struck, all veterans of the hard fighting in Italy. There was strong resistance only in spots and those not numerous, for information provided by the French underground was so accurate that every defense installation had been heavily hit by shells and bombs in the preliminary stages. Indeed, the area of the American landing was found to be held by only two regiments, composed of Poles and Czechs who had been pressed into the German service and who surrendered at the first opportunity. Many similar formations were rounded up by the underground in the rear areas and by the third day of the landing the Allied forces already had over 10,000 prisoners while their own casualties numbered under 2,000.

The French forces pressed rapidly west, masking Toulon and laying siege to Marseille, which fell on August 23 and was found in the same state of wreckage as other port towns captured from the Germans. Toulon was both more defensible and had stronger guns. It was not taken till August 26, after a week of bitter street fighting, also by French forces.

Meanwhile the American VI Corps of General Truscott was rushing through all the gaps toward the broad Rhone Valley, meeting almost no resistance, for in view of the situation further north the Germans had decided to pull out, leaving detachments behind to complicate our supply problem by holding the ports. The decision was made too late and the movement, hampered by the underground and by American aviation, which now had fields in France, was made too slowly. At Montelimar on August 25 General Truscott's men got across the path of an armored division and parts of two others. There was a battle; nearly all the 15,000 Germans were killed or captured and they were forced to abandon 800 tanks.

Patch's columns pushed ahead rapidly, throwing out one wing to connect with the Third Army in the region of Paris on September 15, while another swung around the tip of Swiss territory which juts into France and came up to the Belfort Gap that leads to the plains of Alsace. Their brief campaign had yielded 50,000 prisoners, and the Nineteenth German Army, like the Seventh, had been substantially destroyed.

For Germans the disorganization caused by the Allied victories was less serious than it might have been in other services. Under their system, commands and staffs as far down as the regimental level are purely temporary. When groups as large as a battalion held together they could readily be assembled into new major formations. But the over-all position of the Germans was now thoroughly bad. The failure to hold Patch placed the new left flank of their position along the Seine at the end of August, 1944, in double jeopardy. The core of their forces was made up of the Fifteenth

Army, more properly a group of armies, which had
been largely in the Calais region; there were also
fragments of the Seventh Army and of the First,
which had been holding central France and the
Biscay ports.

The main concentrations were along the Seine
between Paris and Le Havre, with only the slender-
est formations of garrison troops and hastily found
reinforcements east of the French capital. On this
flank our forces had the highly mobile Third Army
of General Patton. He had brought his formations
up to the Seine on both sides of the French city on
August 22, but those to the north and west were
pulled out to fall in behind the rest for a move to
the eastward to get around the weak German flank.
Our First Army took over west of Paris on August 25. General Eisenhower much gratified French
susceptibilities by allowing their Second Armored
Division to be the first group into the city where
they had captured the German garrison, 10,000
strong.

Beyond Paris, Patton crossed the Seine with ease
and lunged north toward Rheims and the Belgian
border, resting his right flank in the highlands of
the Meuse, which river was reached on August 31.
By that date, British, Canadians, and the American First Army all had strong bridgeheads across
the lower Seine and the German High Command
had lost interest in fighting for the retention of

Flanders and the buzz-bomb bases. They threw heavy garrisons into the coastal ports—Calais, Le Havre, Dunkirk, Ostend, Boulogne—and retreated as rapidly as possible, resisting only by means of rear guards, mine fields and demolitions. The situation was now completely fluid, with troops moving rapidly in all directions, but thanks to the superiority of our forces in vehicles and in the air, the Allies had the superior mobility at all times save when the enemy chose to achieve a delay by sacrificing portions of their forces.

Even this did not always work, since the Germans had to swing through a long parabola while the advance could often take short cuts. The VII Corps of the U.S. First Army, moving north from the Aisne crossings, reached Mons by September 3 close on the heels of the retreating enemy. Air scouts brought in the astonishing news that strong German forces were approaching from the southwest in column on the roads. The corps faced around and took position; the enemy were an entire Nazi corps of five divisions, but without air cover and with few tanks. In a savage two-day battle they were surrounded and virtually wiped out; 22,000 prisoners were taken in this most important action of the whole advance.

By September 15, in a rush that has few historical parallels, the British and Canadians were up the line of the Scheldt where it runs west to the

North Sea, and had taken Antwerp, which they found, rather surprisingly, neither destroyed nor defended. From here their line ran southeast to meet that held by the American forces, who had reached a tiny corner of German territory opposite Aachen. From Aachen our line ran south, generally just inside the borders of Luxembourg, to where the Meuse turns northeast for its plunge through the Eiffel Mountains, and from here on south along the Meuse till the mountains of Alsace were reached. The Third Army held some bridge-heads across the Meuse and the Seventh had gained possession of the Belfort Gap, but in general the position had stabilized, the advance had been halted.

There were several reasons for this. One was that the Germans brought in reinforcements from their general reserve while our forces had been subjected to the amount of straggling unavoidable in so rapid an advance. This process was aided by many small pockets of isolated Germans, which had to be mopped up by detachments that later had to be brought back to their parent units, with resulting complication of traffic problems.

The second reason was that the fall rains of northern Europe had begun, and the lowering skies had their usual effect on the Allied air forces. The Germans had a great deal of heavy artillery in the positions to which they had retreated. Our forces

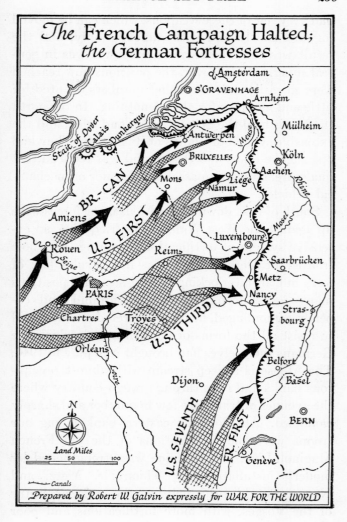

The French Campaign Halted; the German Fortresses

Amsterdam
S'GRAVENHAGE
Arnhem
Mülheim
Strait of Dover
Calais
Dunkerque
Antwerpen
Meuse
Köln
BR-CAN
BRUXELLES
Aachen
Mons
Liège
Namur
Amiens
U.S. FIRST
Rhine
Rouen
Seine
Reims
Luxembourg
Mosel
Saarbrücken
PARIS
Metz
Chartres
Troyes
U.S. THIRD
Nancy
Strasbourg
Orléans
Loire
Belfort
Dijon
Basel
N
U.S. SEVENTH
FR. FIRST
BERN
Land Miles
0 25 50 100
Genève
Canals

Prepared by Robert W. Galvin expressly for WAR FOR THE WORLD

had very few of these weapons, which can be moved forward slowly and with difficulty only, and the result was that the enemy's firepower was in general superior. Moreover, the positions now reached were so easily defensible that numbers counted for little and mobility for almost nothing. In the north the Nazis held the Scheldt, deep and wide, and the extensive system of islands at its mouth. They had opened the dikes and the ground was reduced to a quagmire, almost impassable for armor or mechanical vehicles.

South of this, down to the Meuse, our forces were up against the West Wall, or Siegfried Line, an extensive system of fortifications covering the whole frontier of Germany. It was not a solid line of forts but an interlocking belt of separate positions many miles deep, mostly underground and expertly camouflaged, heavily concreted and designed to resist all the forms of modern attack which the Germans themselves had brought into play in 1940. The Meuse is a deep stream with almost precipitous banks and runs through rough country where the avenues of traffic are few in number and sharply canalized. All along its eastern bank facing our troops were the fortifications of the old French Maginot Line; and this line was strengthened by modern installations at Thionville, Metz, and Nancy. South of this belt was the broken country of the Vosges, with more fortifications and poor lines of communication on the Allied side, very good ones on the German.

But the main reason for the slowing up of the great drive was the question of supply. The abrupt halt of the Third Army, whose tanks had run half across France, is very striking. The Third had run short of both fuel and ammunition after reaching the Meuse, in spite of the fact that a pipeline had been built across the entire English Channel underwater and linked with a great express highway that had been constructed from Normandy to Paris to convey exactly these items up to the front. The French railroads had been systematically raided for rolling stock by the Germans during the occupation and systematically wrecked during the retreat. They could give little help. France had been plucked so clean that even much of the food for its civilian population had to be brought in—an enormous burden in addition to supplying the needs of the armies.

In dealing with this burden there was a serious bottleneck in port facilities. Cherbourg and the artificial harbor at Arromanches were long the only places through which ocean-going ships could be unloaded. Brest, indeed, fell to the attacks of the newly organized Ninth American Army under Lieutenant-General William H. Simpson on September 19; Boulogne was taken by the Canadians on September 18, following their capture of Le

Havre on the 12th. But the demolitions at Boulogne had been so thorough that it was considered impossible to repair the harbor in time to be of any use in this war. The capacity of Boulogne was small and it was the end of the year before Le Havre could be gotten into shape. Marseille, as soon as it was cleared, became a main reliance; 18,000 tons of supplies were moved through it daily, and ultimately 14 divisions of troops were landed there. But the use of Marseille involved a long journey by ships up through the Strait of Gibraltar at one end and a long journey by railroad at the other. The armies at the front continued to develop shortages.

Nevertheless General Eisenhower thought that by pressing the enemy before he had a chance to rally great results might be achieved. The method worked out was for the use of an airborne army under Lieutenant-General L. H. Brereton to turn the West Wall at its northern end. It had been intended to use this army, which consisted of two entire American airborne divisions and one British with a number of special groups, in operations in France, but the advance proved so rapid that an airborne movement was unnecessary. On September 17 the air army was launched in an attempt to gain crossings of the great rivers that flow west through Holland. Carried by nearly 3,000 planes, the 82nd and 101st American divisions were set down near Eindhoven north of the Maas, to gain the bridges. The British were dropped at Arnheim north of the Waal mouth of the Rhine to win the great bridge there. In support of this operation the British Second Army attacked north toward the Scheldt with the design of linking up to the airborne troops.

They had a cloudy day, which made German anti-aircraft weak and ineffective. The two American divisions managed to organize their ground and link up with the Second Army across the Scheldt after several days of severe fighting. But near Arnheim the Germans had two armored divisions in a rest area. As soon as the airborne British landed they were assailed by overwhelming numbers of troops who had plenty of artillery and armor while they had very little. All efforts at relief failed, and after a dogged defense the division was nearly wiped out.

This event and the fact that our armies were everywhere stalled in heavy fighting against strong fortifications sent a wave of pessimism sweeping through the country. While the Germans were breaking across France, the Russians had been making wide gains in the east and it seemed that the Nazis could not hold out much longer. In fact preparations for victory observances had been made in many places. The Germans adroitly aided this overconfidence by means of propaganda em-

phasizing their own despair and urging all citizens
to take up arms, while exaggerating Allied gains by
announcing that such places as Metz and Nancy
had fallen after slight resistance. In addition, just
at this juncture when the clearing of the Channel
coast brought an end to the buzz-bomb attacks,
the Germans appeared with the second and more
terrible of their V-weapons, V-2, a true rocket
which moved in the region of the stratosphere at
such speed that no interception was possible. It
could be fired from North Holland and even from
Germany itself and still hit London. In fact, several dozen a day did hit the city.

The resulting disappointment was considerable,
but it was somewhat misplaced. Actually there was
no longer any question about who was going to
win the war. In the battles across France and the
Lowlands the Nazis had lost well over half a million men, many of them the best troops in the service, more than half of them in the form of prisoners,
which is the most wasteful form of military expenditure since it inflicts no corresponding disabili-
ties on the opponent. Another 150,000 Germans
were locked up in the ports. Their reserve depots
were empty; they were reduced to enlisting youths
of fifteen and old men who had fought in the last
war, to organizing Volksturm battalions of workers
and women who had no military training. In the
east, the Russians had for the first time conducted

a successful summer offensive, which cleared the whole Ukraine, old Poland, and Rumania; they were deep in Hungary on a thousand-mile front that required the full efforts of the depleted German armies merely to hold, and those armies were now back to a line they must maintain in order to keep intact the only remaining industrial areas beyond the range of Allied bombers. Worst of all, the Nazis had been unable to find any commander with the ability and freedom of action of Montgomery of the British, and among the Americans, of Patton, Bradley, and above all Eisenhower, whose campaign from June to September ranks as one of the greatest in military history.

CHAPTER XV

THE operations against Los Negros and Manus Islands of the Admiralty Group, 200 miles south of the great enemy base at Truk, had originally been scheduled for April, 1944, but were pushed up to the last day of February because the Japanese at Kwajalein and Truk, and those in the operations around Vitiaz Strait showed little disposition toward strategic counterattack. Manus was something more than another way station on the road along the New Guinea coast. It has an excellent harbor, well sheltered against weather, and, being remote from any land mass where Japanese bands were still afloat, did not require military operations in the hinterland. It was accordingly erected into a major base for southwest Pacific operations, the navy moving in floating repair shops, floating docks, depot ships and even bakeries afloat, while the army set up similar installations ashore.

Here were established the headquarters of the new Seventh Fleet, an organization headed by

Rear-Admiral Thomas C. Kinkaid, who had commanded in the battle of the Eastern Solomons in August, 1942. The organization was under General MacArthur's command and was intended to furnish naval support for operations primarily military, as Admiral Nimitz had been given four divisions of army troops for attacks on islands where the outlook and effect of the campaign would be fundamentally naval. For the time being, the new fleet consisted of escort carriers with destroyers and cruisers, heavy support being furnished by the fast battleship and carrier task forces from the Central Pacific. The service of information by means of code intercepts and submarine scouting had grown so efficient that there was little opportunity for the enemy to move heavy ships into the Southwest Pacific area without our forces being able to cut them off.

March and most of April, 1944, were spent in organizing the new base at Manus, shifting other base installations from Australia up to the cost of New Guinea, and preparing for the next move forward. This was to be Hollandia, 400 miles along the coast of New Guinea from the deepest previous penetration, an area isolated by a range of mountains that runs down from the central backbone of the island. Hollandia contained three excellent airfields and a harbor that could be erected into an advanced base. In those jungle countries information as to Japanese strength was never wholly reliable and the strategic importance of the place made it likely that the enemy had concentrated there in force. Their Eighteenth Army was known to be in New Guinea and was supposed to be in the Hollandia area some 60,000 strong, with outer elements facing the Australo-American forces just south of Medang. There was an extensive barge traffic along the shore which we never had been able to cut off completely, though our light forces sank as many as a hundred of these craft a month.

General MacArthur detailed all three divisions of Lieutenant-General R. L. Eichelberger's I Corps for the operation and, as it fell in the time gap of Central Pacific operations between the taking of Eniwetok and the major move against the Marianas, he besought the services of the fast carriers for air support. The operation was thus the most massive that had yet been undertaken in the Southwest Pacific. Cruisers and destroyers fired the preliminary bombardment on the night of April 21–22; after dawn on the latter day landing forces moved in simultaneously against the beaches of Aitape and of Hollandia itself, preceded by intense fire from rocket-gunboats.

Resistance was surprisingly light at both places. By April 23 all the airfields were in American hands and our fighters were being set up on the Aitape air strip. The forces at the two landings worked toward each other in a move to encircle the Japanese between coast and mountains, but only about a company of the enemy were cut off and exterminated. Their force had been overestimated; the rest of the less than five thousand men the area really held were driven off into the hills where most perished miserably without affecting the course of the war.

It was now clear that the majority of the New Guinea Japanese were in the Wewak area, but they were comparatively harmless there, blocked off from undertaking operations by the very combination of mountain and jungle that preserved them from landward attack. MacArthur began organizing his Hollandia base while some detachments pushed into the hills in pursuit of the Japanese there and others moved along the coast 75 miles to the next enemy station at the offshore island of Wakde, on which a landing was effected May 17. There was the usual fanatic resistance, overwhelmed with light casualties, for MacArthur had put in nearly an entire brigade against the single battalion of Japanese who held the island.

The next blow was made against Biak Island on May 27 by the 41st Division. The landing was made without opposition, but as our troops began to work along the coast road they ran into violent machine-gun and artillery fire from a line of bluffs, and were counterattacked by numbers of tanks supported by infantry. Heavy fighting lasted nearly a week; extra ships and planes had to be brought in to support the beachhead and it became evident that Biak was much more important in the Japanese scheme of military economy than had been supposed. The forces against the Japanese were too powerful, however; their formal resistance began to break on June 3. On June 6 one of the airfields was reached and after that it was merely a question of digging the remnants of the 8,000 enemy troops out of cave positions like those on Saipan.

Early in July there was another landing at Noemfor on the Vogelkop Peninsula in extreme west New Guinea, followed on July 30 by one at Sansapor, farther down the same peninsula. Both of these caught the enemy off balance and achieved their objectives with light loss. The New Guinea campaign that had begun in June, 1943, was now complete except for peripheral operations against the Japanese still in the hills there, and at Wewak, where a daily bombing and shelling from the sea became the rule. The separate steps of this campaign have little of military interest and were much alike—the swift rush of overwhelming forces to an obscure beach, the hard labor to hack an air strip out of the jungle, the assembly of troops and supplies for the next move. The real heroes of the campaign were the medical and supply officers, and the planners who achieved surprise against the enemy with a regularity that was almost monotonous. In a little over a year they had changed into a chain of American bases an area, 1,400 miles long and occupied by nearly 250,000 enemy troops.

THOSE Japanese on Vogelkop Peninsula who escaped our attack retreated to the south face of the island on Banda Sea and were evacuated by boat. It was mid-August of 1944 before they were cleared out and the new air strip at Sansapor brought into full commission—about the same date that saw Guam reconquered and the new bases in the Marianas operative. The conjunction of events brought strategic considerations to the fore. Up to this time the navy in the Central Pacific and General MacArthur in the South Pacific had conducted their campaigns independently save when the fleet was borrowed for some such operation as that against Hollandia. It is probable that the navy would have preferred to continue this arrangement. General MacArthur had a well-known predilection for a return to the Philippines and a campaign there to by-pass Japanese holdings in the Dutch Indies. This would have the ancillary result of permitting American naval operations in the South China Sea and so cutting off the enemy's access to his sources of supply in the south except by the undeveloped and uncertain overland route through China.

The navy on the other hand would undoubtedly have preferred a campaign to cut off the Japanese lifeline more thoroughly and nearer the home islands at Formosa or some point in the Ryukyus, looking forward to a landing on the Chinese coast. But any conceivable move in that direction would involve a military campaign on a land mass of some size and would require many troops. MacArthur headed the only considerable body of troops in the South Pacific, and both for political reasons (it was a Presidential year) and the sentimental purpose of bringing aid to the Philippines at the earliest opportunity, the Joint Chiefs of Staff in Washington allowed the General's viewpoint to prevail. Troops and fleet were to operate together against the Philippines.

Troops and fleet had, however, swung far apart since the Solomons campaign. If the Philippines were to be attacked, it was necessary to bring them together again in an area where the expedition could be made up with reasonable security from enemy observation and where the fleet would still be in position to cover the new Central Pacific bases against any counterattack by Japanese mobile forces. Between our two commands stretched the vast belt of the Carolines, still held by the enemy in strength. Truk at its core was continually reinforced by airplanes staged out through the Philippines, and was itself used by the Japanese reconnaissance planes that came down to look at the easternmost projection of MacArthur's advance.

These considerations fixed the point for the next offensive in the western Carolines. A base seized there would be even more forward than Sansapor and would be necessary for any attack on the Philippines. It was decided to take two bases. The MacArthur forces would attack Morotai off Halmahera, the air gate to the Indies, and the navy forces, simultaneously giving cover to the Morotai attack, would fall on Ulithi and the Palau group, then move on Yap. Halsey was placed in command of the forces afloat, which were again denominated the Third Fleet. Kinkaid remained attached to MacArthur, but with greatly augmented forces, which included most of the slow battleships available. They could be spared from the Third Fleet which now had eight of the new fast battleships in service with two more running their shakedown cruises.

The operations began on September 5 with a massive carrier strike against the Palaus, while cruisers and escort carriers of Halsey's command moved on Ulithi. The latter found no Japanese at the place and as it had an admirable sheltered lagoon it was decided to put the navy's train (floating base) in there. Meanwhile the cruisers and escort carriers pushed on to pick up the bombardment of the Palaus where the fast battleships had left off, while the latter in turn moved on to give Morotai "the Halsey haircut," and then swung southwestward to attack the airfields in the eastern Philippines, from which the Japanese might be expected to attempt to support the areas now under pressure.

On the morning of September 8, Halsey's planes struck the fields of Mindanao. The Japanese warning system failed completely, many of their planes were caught on the ground, and off the coast they lost a whole convoy of ships. Halsey pounded the area for another day, then ran on to strike the air installations of Luzon. This time the Japanese were warned, for they had developed a radar system which gave them some service. There were air fights over the fields and over Manila harbor for two days; but if their information service had improved since our people last made contact with the Japanese, their aviation had gained nothing. From their scattered and inefficiently operated fields they could send up little to match the squadrons of nearly twenty carriers. As Halsey turned eastward on September 12, he left behind him the wreckage of nearly 2,000 Japanese planes. That night he sent through an urgent message suggesting that, since the Japanese proved so very weak in the Philippines, the attack on Yap be dropped out of the picture and the invasion of the islands be begun as soon as Morotai and the Palaus were secure—a reversal of the original plan, which had been to invade after the winter rains were over.

THERE was a series of rapid-fire, long-range conferences, in which Nimitz offered MacArthur the services of three army divisions (the 7th, 77th, and 96th) under navy control, for an immediate invasion. The approval of the Joint Chiefs of Staff was secured for the project. MacArthur had expected to have air support from Chennault's 14th Air Force in South China. He was now informed that this was impossible since the Japanese had taken the bases, but the carriers made themselves responsible for air cover till the General could win fields for his own air force, the 5th. With this background MacArthur agreed to speed up the invasion. It placed a burden of incredible weight and complexity upon the staff planners who had so well handled the New Guinea campaign, and it may be said that, if the fate of the German war depended on Eisenhower's Normandy invasion, the result of the Japanese war was now wedded to this move.

The two new island invasions had taken place on September 15, 1944, while the matter was still being discussed, and furnished somewhat contradictory indications as to the possibilities of success. The actual landing on Morotai was unopposed. The Japanese had evidently expected a move to the shores of Halmahera across the strait and were disposed at the wrong place. The campaign thus consisted in hunting down a few scattered bands. The attack on the Palaus was directed against the two southernmost islands of the chain, Angaur and Peleliu. Part of the 81st Division attacked the former, the 1st Marine Division the latter, and it was assumed that if these two were gained, the larger islands of the group could be controlled from their air strips. Angaur was believed to be held by not more than a company of Japanese; Peleliu, by about 4,500 men.

The method was the same as that applied in the Marshalls. Carriers, battleships, and cruisers subjected the place to intensive bombardment for over a week before landing day. At Angaur the fighting was sharp but brief; in three days the island was clear. But Angaur lies outside the coral rim enclosing the atoll and has no harbor of its own. It was necessary to have Peleliu, and at Peleliu the Japanese demonstrated that their defensive techniques had caught up with our methods of attack. The island is a high structure of coral limestone honeycombed with caves; the Japanese had added to these and had built an intricate system of tunnels, linking cave to cave. The preliminary bombardments had hurt them very little. When the Marines hit the beach they were met by a storm of fire from pieces of all sizes which pinned them down at once; they were then subjected to a tank-led counterattack that broke through one of our regiments.

It was far worse than the more publicized Tarawa operation, for each individual cave had to be cleared out in hand-to-hand fighting, and often enough the Japanese reoccupied the cave later by means of their interior tunnels. One of the Marine regiments lost two thirds of its numbers, the 81st Division had to be called on for help, and two months after the landing men were still being killed by snipers hidden underground.

This was clearly an instance of underestimating the enemy's strength and resources. On the other hand, it proved that Halsey had by no means underestimated their strength and resources in the air. After the Luzon strike, his fast ships ran up to the Marianas for a brief period of refueling and refitting and then turned into the Western Pacific toward the region of the Ryukyus and Formosa, the design being to knock out the planes with which the Philippines could be supported while those planes were still distributed among the reserve fields.

Halsey struck the fields of the southern Ryukyus on October 9, getting rid of a hundred Japanese machines and butchering a couple of small convoys without appreciable loss before he went on to strike the great bases of Formosa on the 11th, an attack repeated the following day. The Japanese were comparatively well prepared. In a heavy air battle we lost 50 planes against 180 of theirs, and inflicted considerable damage on their shops and installations. That night they called in planes from the China coast or brought them out of underground hangars on Formosa and counterattacked the fleet; a night torpedo attack made in great force.

Against our night-fighter patrols and the gunfire of the fleet they succeeded in getting exactly one hit on a heavy cruiser, which was dragged home clear across the Pacific. But the determining factor of the battle was that, when shot down, the enemy planes exploded with such enormous violence among pillars of flame that many even of our own fighters thought several carriers had been blown up. The Japanese thoroughly believed it. Their messages (which we were decoding) announced the destruction of 11 American carriers.

Now Halsey's major concern was the Japanese fleet, and he believed he might persuade them out for a battle if he encouraged their delusion that they had destroyed so much of our carrier strength. Accordingly he turned south and east beyond range of Japanese scouts toward the Palaus with three of his four carrier groups. The fourth, that of Rear-Admiral J. S. McCain, was left hovering in the great bight of ocean between Formosa and the

Philippines, flying a strike next morning against the fields of northern Luzon. McCain was duly attacked by torpedo planes again that night and the Japanese raised their count of American carriers sunk to fourteen. But they did not bring their fleet out and Halsey believed that his ruse had failed.

Now he ran down to join the Seventh Fleet in escorting the MacArthur armada, already on the water, toward the Philippines. At the last moment its destination had been changed from Mindanao, the point originally selected, to Leyte. The extremely active and well-informed guerrilla movement in the islands (it was supported by American submarines) sent out word that the Japanese had concentrated to the north and south of the Philippine group, leaving the central islands almost uncovered. On October 19, 1944, a Japanese search plane spotted the Seventh Fleet and the transports as they approached Leyte Gulf. On the 20th the landings began under cover of naval fire and rocket ships so effective that the first men on the beach (of the 1st Cavalry Division) penetrated half a mile into the jungles before they had a single casualty. General MacArthur returned to the Philippines during the morning, and army formations began to extend perimeters inland around the airstrips of Tacloban (Leyte's capital) and Dulag, on which work began immediately. The Japanese resistance was light but persistent in that tangled country; the advance progressed slowly under cover of planes from the 18 escort carriers of Rear-Admiral Thomas Sprague, part of the Seventh Fleet. But before the military movements could attain the proportions of a campaign a new factor had entered the situation.

The Japanese fleet decided to fight. Halsey's stratagem had really deceived them, and when Rear-Admiral F. C. Sherman appeared in the bight of Luzon with a single carrier group on the 21st, the Japanese Admiral, Kurita, assumed it was the same group that had attacked Luzon on the 13th (McCain's) and that these were all the fast carriers we had left. The Japanese gunnery ships were in the region of Singapore; Kurita brought them north at speed along the western side of the Philippines. Two battleships, one heavy cruiser, and some light cruisers and destroyers were to run through the Sulu Sea into Surigao Strait and Leyte Gulf to attack our transports and beachheads. Five battleships, seven heavy cruisers, and a host of lighter craft were to run east through Sibuyan Sea and San Bernardino Strait, round Samar and so reach the same destination. Another cruiser and destroyer force was to start from the north through the Sulu Sea, and thence into Surigao Strait.

A force of 200 bombers, many of them suddenly

flown in from China, were to fly from the Luzon
fields and strike Sherman, while four carriers, all
that was left of that once great wing of the Japanese navy, with two battleships and many smaller
craft, ran down from the region of the Japanese
islands, well to the east. They were to fly their
planes across Sherman's ships, attacking as they
passed, to the landing fields of Luzon, then shuttle
back across the carriers again, to be picked up at
sea. These carriers were expected to be lost in de-
coying our ships away from Leyte Gulf. Finally,
the Japanese had organized a corps of pilots sworn
to dive into American ships with full bomb loads.
These—the Kamikaze—would attack the remnants
of the Seventh Fleet while Kurita's battleships were
pounding it.

This was the plan, many details of which did
not become clear to our side till much later. The
first word the American leaders had was on the
night of October 23, when our submarines *Darter*
and *Dace*, scouting off Dumaron Channel south of
Palawan, sighted Kurita's armada bound north.
They got the news off and attacked. In the most
successful submarine action of the whole war they
sank two of the Japanese heavy cruisers and sent
a third back to Singapore with four torpedo holes
in her. Halsey immediately moved his carrier
groups up to a point east of Samar and at dawn
on the 24th flew off search and strike groups. One

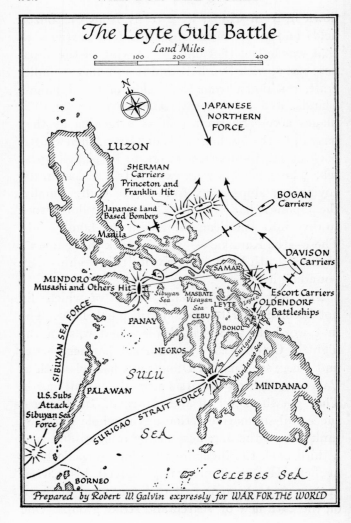

The Leyte Gulf Battle

Land Miles

0   100   200   400

JAPANESE
NORTHERN
FORCE

LUZON

SHERMAN
Carriers
Princeton and
Franklin Hit

BOGAN
Carriers

Japanese Land
Based Bombers

DAVISON
Carriers

Manila

SAMAR

Escort Carriers

MINDORO
Musashi and Others Hit

Sibuyan
Sea

MASBATE
Visayan
Sea
CEBU

LEYTE

Leyte

OLDENDORF
Battleships

PANAY

BOHOL

Surigao Sea

NEGROS

SULU

Mindanao Sea

U.S. Subs
Attack
Sibuyan Sea
Force

PALAWAN

SURIGAO STRAIT FORCE

MINDANAO

SEA

BORNEO

CELEBES SEA

SIBUYAN SEA FORCE

Prepared by Robert W. Galvin expressly for WAR FOR THE WORLD

of the strikes found a Japanese formation proceeding through Sulu Sea and inflicted some damage on it, but before a second strike could be flown all planes were called to the northern end of the area, where the much more important Japanese force was steaming through Sibuyan Sea and Sherman's carrier group had been attacked by the land-based bombers. Sherman beat off these attackers with the loss of nearly a hundred enemy planes, but not before they had left the light carrier *Princeton* furiously ablaze and had scored a hit on another carrier. He could give no help against the Japanese battleships.

The other carrier groups attacked this force all day, concentrating on the biggest ships, and cutting them up very badly. In the final attack just at twilight they set upon the battleship *Musashi*, newest and finest of the Japanese navy, hitting her so heavily that she sank before another dawn, though our people did not know it at the time. They were satisfied to see this battle force turning west, back in the direction from which it had come.

Meanwhile Sherman's hard-pressed carriers had been attacked by the Japanese planes coming in from their carriers out to seaward. The *Princeton* blew up and almost wrecked the light cruiser *Birmingham*, which was helping her to put out fires. The Japanese suffered considerably from our air groups but a good portion of them got away.

So stood the situation on the night of October 24, 1944. One Japanese squadron was making through the Sulu Sea toward Surigao Strait at its best speed, with another coming to join it, the two admirals ignorant of each other. In the northern end of that strait, though the enemy did not know it, waited Rear-Admiral J. L. Oldendorf with six battleships of Kinkaid's command (five of them ships that had gone down at Pearl Harbor) and numerous cruisers and destroyers. In the Sibuyan Sea the main Japanese battle force was turning back after a dreadful battering from our carrier planes. On the Luzon fields, Japanese land-based and carrier bombers were reloading for another attack on Sherman's group, which they apparently still supposed were all the carriers we had left. Somewhere out to the north and east, not yet definitely located, was the Japanese carrier force with accompanying battleships.

During the night a long-range search plane from the Marianas found them, and Halsey turned toward them with his whole force. Some critics complained later that he had not left part of the ships to hold San Bernardino Strait, but it was old American tactical doctrine never to divide a fleet in the presence of an enemy. It will also be remembered that no one on the American side yet knew how extensive the Japanese losses in the June battle (Philippine Sea) had been. Instead of its actual size of one large and three light carriers, this Japanese force might easily have contained five of each type, and if so, it was by far the most formidable opponent. Halsey hurried toward it through the dark at his best speed. The decoy thus was a success.

In that same dark at about 3:00 A.M. the southernmost Japanese force entered Surigao Strait. Oldendorf had disposed his battleship across the exit of the strait with cruisers and destroyers down both sides. As soon as his radar showed the enemy steaming straight on in line ahead, his destroyers let loose shoals of torpedoes and the heavy ships opened up a torrent of gunfire rarely seen in war —*Tennessee* alone fired 69 shells of a ton weight and 63 of them hit. In twelve minutes the entire Japanese squadron was reduced to a group of floating wrecks, with damage to only one of the destroyers on our side. A little later the second enemy force arrived and was as badly hurt.

But still worse was in store for the Japanese. At daybreak Halsey's planes found the carrier force. Its planes (as we have seen) had left it to fly into Luzon and no defense remained but anti-aircraft fire with which to oppose the heaviest carrier attack yet seen in the Pacific. One of their carriers went down under that first blow. All the rest of the ships were more or less badly hit and turned to race back toward Japan as fast as they were able.

But before a second strike could be flown to finish them, before the American battleships could close in with their big guns, the radio brought Halsey an appalling piece of news. The Japanese Sibuyan Sea force, with which he thought he had finished, had turned again during the night, speeded up, burst through San Bernardino Strait, and now had Sprague's escort carriers under its guns, with Leyte Gulf, crowded with transports, only a little beyond.

It seemed that nothing could save those escort carriers. They were armorless and slow, converted from merchant hulls. Their only cover was a handful of destroyers and destroyer escorts. The range was point blank. Oldendorf was far distant, with slow ships now nearly out of both fuel and ammunition. The destroyers and destroyer escorts made smoke screens and gallantly attacked with the torpedo. Three of them (*Johnston, Hoel, Roberts*) were sunk, and the escort carrier *Gambier Bay* took an engine-room hit that caused her to drop back among the onrushing Japanese and go down under their gunfire. But all the Japanese ships had been severely battered by carrier planes the day before and this damage had fallen particularly upon their upper works where range finders and fire-control instruments were located. Their gunnery was wretched. Moreover, the escort carriers themselves were by no means helpless. Their own planes took off to fall on the Japanese in attack after attack. In one of these rushes they sank the heavy cruiser *Suzuyu* with seven torpedo hits and hit another cruiser so badly that she was forced to turn away. At about 9:30, after two hours of firing, being short of ammunition and having suffered dismaying losses, the rest of the Japanese imitated her, realizing that before they could finish the escort carriers Halsey and his whole armada would be down on them.

Halsey had indeed turned back, leaving Admiral Mitscher with one group of carriers to complete the work on the Japanese force in the north, but rejecting the latter's plea to give him a couple of battleships, the only action for which the American fleet commander can really be blamed. His planes ran ahead to the neighborhood of Samar. Sometime around noon or a little after, they charged head on into the few remaining Japanese carrier planes coming out from Luzon to rejoin their own fleet, of whose disaster they had not yet heard. The enemy were in no condition to combat the overwhelming American fighter groups and were nearly all shot down.

About the same time the Kamikaze attacked the escort carriers, just delivered from the Japanese battleships, and though most were shot down, one of them did crash through the deck of the escort carrier *St. Lo*, setting fires that could not be checked. Halsey's air-strike groups pressed on, hitting the Japanese now in flight through San Bernardino Strait and slowing them up enough so that our battleships caught one or two ships and finished them off. In the north, Mitscher's men flew two more major strikes against the Japanese carrier group fleeing for home. All their carriers were sunk and all their other ships crippled. In the night an American submarine got one of their cruisers; for three days more our carrier planes hunted all over the Philippines, finding and sinking damaged destroyers, and within the week two more injured heavy cruisers had been sent down in the bays of Luzon where they had taken refuge.

That was the Battle of Leyte Gulf, the greatest in American naval history. In that confused series of actions the Japanese carrier service had been wiped out, together with 392 airplanes; three of their battleships had been sunk; they had lost eight of their twelve heavy cruisers (two after the battle itself), five light cruisers and nine destroyers—more than half their navy, which never again operated as a fleet, for the remaining five battleships and four heavy cruisers were badly hurt. To the war in the Pacific, Leyte was what St. Lô-Avranches had been to the war in Europe—the crushing blow. After it, the enemy could have no higher hope than a negotiated peace which would leave them some fragments of their empire.

CHAPTER XVI

ECONQUEST OF THE PHILIPPINES

As captured documents later showed, the Japanese were completely deceived by General MacArthur's landing on Leyte in October, 1944. They had expected a two-pronged attack—from the Central Pacific forces under Nimitz against northern Luzon and from MacArthur's men at Mindanao. The virtual destruction of their fleet in Leyte Gulf accordingly left them in very poor position, without any good means of assembling at the point of contact the 350,000 men who formed the garrison of the islands.

Their commander, Terauchi, nevertheless decided to fight for Leyte, since the island's central mountain range had few passes and they could be held by relatively small forces. Where the country was open it was largely in rice paddies, and the season of torrential rains was at hand. These were all factors that favored a static defense and cut down American mobility, while the water channels among the islands west of Leyte were narrow

enough to permit considerable supporting movement in small craft by night, when our aviation was
least effective. (The fact that both Japanese and
Germans were forced to seek positions from which
American mobility could be discounted was not
accidental but the product of two perfectly measurable military factors, the exceptional power of
movement conferred on our forces by their automotive equipment, which could bring supplies up so
rapidly, and the operations of our air force, which
made rapid movement so difficult for the opponents.)

General MacArthur's problem was the converse
of the Japanese—to break out rapidly from the area
in which he was penned between the beach and
mountains of Leyte and, using the strategic mobility conferred by our command of the sea, to deal
with the enemy forces in detail. He had six divisions in the Sixth Army of General Kreuger—not
over 100,000 men—with the support of General
Kenney's Fifth Air Force after the Dulag and Tacloban strips were set up and others added. General
Walter Kreuger had already demonstrated, and
would so again, that he was one of the ablest American commanders anywhere in the field; he was a
German immigrant, gifted with wonderful persistence, a skillful tactician whose greatest recommen-
dation was nevertheless not tactics but his control
of morale by living like his soldiers and treating

their problems as his own. "We all command armies," he told a meeting of sergeants once, "the only difference being that mine is larger than yours." He also had the support of Halsey's planes from the fast carriers, which were used for this purpose because practically all the Seventh Fleet escort carriers had been disabled in the battle of October 24–25.

Four days after that date, on October 29, the plain of eastern Leyte had been cleared to the mountains and the 1st Cavalry Division had secured the southern tip of Samar, where it abuts on that plain across a very narrow strait. In frantic efforts to hold the American forces back, the Japa-

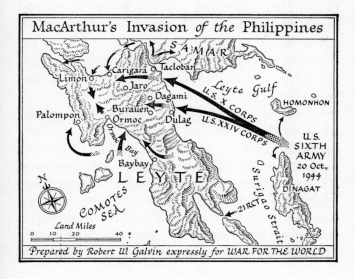

MacArthur's Invasion of the Philippines

Prepared by Robert W. Galvin expressly for WAR FOR THE WORLD

nese had spent a whole division, wiped out in piece-meal attacks with over 14,000 killed, while our casualties were under 3,000. The X Corps of the Sixth Army now moved to the north coast to get around the mountains by one of the two good roads at that flank, while the XXIV Corps took a road through a good pass southward leading to Baybay. It was slow and difficult work at both ends of the line, thanks to the continual rains, but the Japanese were too inferior at every point of contact to make a really good defense, and by November 2 the XXIV Corps had broken through to Baybay with a foothold on the west coast.

By this time the enemy had set up his base at Ormoc farther north on the same coast and had ele-ments of four divisions in there, one of them their 1st Division, supposed to be the very best in the Japanese service; their presence made it clear that the Japanese were committing themselves to a cam-paign for Leyte. All the enemy divisions had suf-fered considerably from the attacks of our planes while on the water, and now their reinforcements began to suffer still more. The capture of Baybay made it possible to base American destroyers and PT-boats in Ormoc Bay and to attack their convoys by night as well as day. This service was not ac-complished without loss to our side, for at night, free from the attentions of American fighters, the Japanese planes attacked constantly. But the enemy lost so heavily in troops that they had difficulty building up large-scale organizations and were constantly forced to expend men and materials in local emergency operations that achieved no more than small-area delays. The disorganization became so pronounced that MacArthur's headquarters somewhat prematurely announced on November 7 that another two weeks would see the island won.

At the end of November the X Corps had taken Limon at the head of the valley which leads south to Ormoc, but the XXIV Corps, moving up from the south toward Ormoc, was substantially halted at a defensible river line, and a division that had attempted to work across the island in the center by mountain trails was making little progress. MacArthur got his 77th Division into light transports and, after a violent air-sea combat that lasted all the night of December 6–7, put them ashore in Ormoc Bay, just north of the Japanese-held river line. This broke up the enemy positions in both directions, and though they did a good deal of damage by dropping suicide parachutists onto our airfields on the night of December 8 their forces rapidly dissolved. On December 21 the last organized resistance broke. The total enemy casualty list was 55,000 men, all but 493 of them killed; our casualties were 11,000. Obscure, semi-guerrilla fighting continued among the hills for nearly six months more, in the course of which another 22,000 Japanese were killed, almost none surrendering. Marshal Terauchi fled to Saigon in Indo-China.

On December 13, 1944, after it became evident that the Ormoc Bay landing would succeed in breaking down the enemy on Leyte, a force of transports under heavy naval escort carried a combat team, two regiments strong, right through the Central Philippines to the coast of Mindoro, the large island just south of Luzon. They rapidly gained all essential areas without meeting any Japanese force of more than constabulary strength. The operation was both an experiment and a preparation; the former because the convoy had to move through narrow waters after having been observed from the outset by the enemy, the latter because it was necessary to establish a forward base before undertaking the invasion of Luzon, most important of the Philippine islands.

The Japanese attacked the convoy continuously from the air during the two nights it was on the water, but all through the month of November Kenney's air force had been hammering at their installations throughout the central islands and the damage inflicted on the convoy was insignificant. The way was accordingly clear for the main attack. It was preceded by a series of feints that succeeded in persuading the Japanese commander that Mac-

The Luzon Campaign

Prepared by Robert W. Galvin expressly for WAR FOR THE WORLD

Arthur meant to land in the Batangas area south of Manila. Mine sweepers moved into the bays there and cleared them out under heavy gunnery cover, planes dropped dummies to simulate an airborne invasion, and several times transports moved in. Meanwhile Filipino guerrillas and the air forces vigorously attacked transportation bottlenecks on Luzon at bridges and ravines. This campaign of confusion was highly successful, for the Japanese, both deceived and uncertain, suffered serious road jams, parceled out their strength needlessly, and had neither good defenses at the shore nor centralized reserves when the real blow fell. With the exception of a single division at some distance, every unit of the close to 200,000 men the Japanese had in the island was on the march in some direction on January 9, 1945, when our troops hit the beach.

The place was the east shore of Lingayen Gulf. The units were of the Sixth Army, now composed of the I and XIV Corps with a completely different list of divisions than when, as nominally the same force, it had struck the beaches of Leyte. The gunnery support was provided by all the vessels of the Seventh Fleet and most of those of the Third Fleet. This proved to be nothing less than necessary, for as the ships moved into Lingayen Gulf it became clear that there was more than one reason why the Japanese aerial counterattacks had tapered off earlier. They had withdrawn many of their planes from service to convert them into Kamikaze, the suicide attackers, and as these planes were not expected to return, they could be operated from otherwise inefficient and easily concealed air strips.

The Kamikaze began their attacks on January 6, as soon as the invasion fleet of over 800 vessels was in easy range. They came in at twilight or dawn in groups close to the water, so that the protecting fighters found it difficult to deal with them and there was some danger of hitting our own ships with gunfire. The attacks were made in unexpected strength and so achieved considerable results. An escort carrier was sunk, and also three mine sweepers. So many other vessels were damaged with great loss of life that the abandonment of the whole operation was seriously considered. Instead Halsey took his Third Fleet north for a great strike on Formosa, hitting the airfields there so effectively that there was little interference with the actual process of landing except from a few pieces of light artillery, easily disposed of.

Once the troops began to reach shore the picture began to change rapidly and radically. The Japanese, like the Germans before them, expected our forces to strike first for one of the ports. They were, therefore, caught so badly out of position that by twilight of the first day 68,000 men were ashore on a beachhead 15 miles long and three miles deep. The flanks were extended rapidly in both directions, but it was January 15 before any important enemy forces were found, and these on the extreme northeastern flank around Rosario, where the Japanese brought up a few pieces of heavy artillery to shell the beachhead from long range. General MacArthur put his weight out toward this flank and succeeded in getting a strong grip on both the main highways that led from Manila up the central valley of Luzon before the two divisions the Japanese had sent north could arrive.

The Japanese by the middle of January did succeed in getting a considerable force into the hill country east of this main valley, their heaviest concentration being on the north flank. This was fairly close to the landing beaches across which our forces were still getting their supplies. The American General put his I Corps out to this flank among the foothills to prevent any counterattack against his communications, and with his XIV Corps pushed rapidly south along the valley toward Manila. It was expected that the enemy would make a stand in the highly defensible position where the River Agno swings a big bend across the valley. Preparations were made for a battle at that point. The event showed that the confusion of Japanese councils and the disarray of their communications had been underestimated rather than the reverse, and MacArthur's advance through the central plain found only weak rear guards at the

Agno. The first heavy fighting came at Clark Field on January 25. The Japanese were found strongly dug in around the field itself and even more firmly entrenched in the hills behind it, from which they could keep the field under artillery fire and prevent its use.

General MacArthur accordingly had to send a considerable force westward into the Zambales Mountains, as he had previously thrust the whole I Corps eastward, where it had encountered strong resistance and was several times counterattacked during January. But these counterattacks were local and piecemeal, and the American leader gave his opponents no time to assemble a mass of maneuver that might take advantage of the weakening of his main column by detachments to the flanks.

On January 9 he put the XI Corps of the Eighth Army ashore on the west coast of Bataan Peninsula near Subic Bay, from whence they pushed rapidly across the peninsula to link up with and to strengthen the main drive. Two days later the 11th Airborne Division went ashore at Nasugbu on Batangas Peninsula south of Manila. When the Japanese attempted to move forces forward to hold off this new attack, the 11th leapfrogged over them in a parachute movement on February 4 and cut these forces off. That same day advance elements of the I Corps reached the northern outskirts of Manila, and now from all directions our troops came pouring down to close the circuit, laying the place under effective siege by February 7.

THE campaign for Luzon was over by February of 1945, but the fighting had hardly begun. The skill of MacArthur's deceptions and the swiftness of his moves were aided enormously by sure information from the Philippine guerrillas as to every Japanese disposition, and also by our command of the sea, which enabled him to strike anywhere in a country whose lines of communication all run close to the water. As a result of these factors, the Japanese were left without a strategy. They were condemned to a defense which consisted in assembling troops in the roughest ground near their stations and waiting to be attacked.

After the American forces closed around Manila on February 7, our troops faced four such main groups, of varying size. The most important was in the mountains of the bulging northern peninsula, now under attack along its perimeter by troops of the I Corps. A somewhat smaller but still important groupment was holding out in the Zambales Mountains and Bataan Peninsula, west of the central valley of Luzon; a third was in the hills around Fort McKinley east of Manila. All three of these were fairly active and made frequent local counterattacks, but were limited to night operations by the presence of our light planes which flew constantly over their positions at tree-top level, bringing down artillery fire on everything that moved.

The fourth concentration was in Manila city itself, with a strong garrison on Corregidor rock in the bay, and it was toward this that General Mac-Arthur first directed his attention, partly because of the moral importance of the place, but principally to gain the use of Manila harbor. Three divisions were put in against the city itself, while two more attacked the forces in the mountains eastward. The latter made good progress at the beginning, cutting all of the communications between the enemy force here and the one in northern Luzon.

The fighting in Manila turned into a desperate inch-by-inch, house-to-house struggle, in which the Japanese killed many of the native inhabitants, mined everything, and made frequent suicide charges on a small scale. By February 21 the area north of the Pasig River, which splits Manila in half, had been cleared and General MacArthur announced that the city was ours. The announcement was premature because the Japanese had dug themselves into the old walled stone city south of the river. A major operation by the full strength of two divisions, with enormous air and artillery support, was necessary to dislodge them, a task not accomplished till the end of the month. The city was left in ruins, without sanitary facilities **or** utilities; great difficulty was experienced in preventing epidemics.

Meanwhile, Bataan had been cleared by the 38th Division, which landed at the tip of the peninsula on February 15 and worked rapidly around the north shore of Manila Bay. Corregidor, under intense bombardment since January 23, fell on February 16 to a parachute attack, admirably timed to arrive at the same moment as a seaborne landing. The remaining Japanese defenders blew themselves up in the tunnels of the Rock to a number never accurately determined; over 4,000 bodies were found aboveground. Another island fortress, Fort Drum, was too small and rugged to be attacked by such means and the Japanese in the place were not eliminated until ships moved up and pumped into its structure vast quantities of gasoline which was then set afire.

From this point on, the fighting on Luzon becomes somewhat obscure because all its separate battles were on a small scale and lacking in interest except to the men who fought in them. Both in the Zambales Mountains and east of Manila the Japanese succeeded in getting into positions ʃith systems of interconnecting caves not unlike those on Peleliu. The position east of Manila was particularly difficult and irritating, since from it the enemy controlled the water reservoirs which constituted the city's supply. Although General MacArthur wanted this and some of the other positions badly enough to make certain sacrifices, there was no such immediate urgency as that which had made the bloody attacks on Peleliu and Saipan a necessity. The war therefore proceeded slowly, on an almost purely tactical level, with the elimination of each position being treated as a separate engineering problem.

In the solution of these problems the most general method was to work men forward to seal the mouth of each cave with explosive charges. Most of the country was too rough for the use of tanks. Artillery fire, rockets, and the new recoilless gun were constantly used to provide covering fire. The Japanese retorted by constant small-scale counterattacks and a campaign of harassments. In spite of the hopelessness of their position, they almost never surrendered. Their efforts were directed toward wearing out the patience of our soldiers and inflicting more casualties on us than they themselves suffered. In the first of these objectives they achieved some success, as later events were to demonstrate, though none that affected the war. The second attempt was an abject failure. General MacArthur's orders to his operations officers were that no attack was to be attempted unless it gave fair promise of ten Japanese casualties for every American. This was not always attained, since our forces occasionally met surprises in the strength or nature of an enemy position, but the actual figure seldom passed below five for one.

In fighting of this character all the east and south of Luzon were cleared during the spring and Baguio was taken, the summer capital and the only place where the Japanese attempted a formal battle. In June, General Kreuger's forces drove into the wide Cagayan Valley, which splits northern Luzon in half. Parachute forces, Philippine guerrillas, and a seaborne attack took Aparri on the north coast, cutting the Japanese from their last contact with the homeland even by submarine and, driving southward, split the remainder of the enemy into pockets.

The supporting fleet had suffered badly during a typhoon in September, 1944, when three destroyers foundered and many other ships were damaged. As soon as Manila Bay was opened to provide a secure anchorage where an expedition could be organized without the necessity of carrying it across Pacific distances, the attack was spread to the other islands of the archipelago. This movement opened on the last day of February, when a combat team from the 41st Division attacked Puerto Princessa on Palawan, the best harbor in the southwestern Philippines. They took it from light opposition, most of the Japanese retreating to the interior hills. Early in April other detachments of the same division took Jolo and Tawitawi in the extreme southern

Philippines, the objective being to gain the key harbors at this end of the vast Philippine group and to cut off from the enemy whatever fitful communication, by means of a small craft, he still had with Borneo and the Japanese-held islands to the south.

On March 10 still another team of the 41st made a beginning on the great island of Mindanao, with a landing at Zamboanga at its extreme western tip. There was hard fighting there, but as on Palawan the matter was not pushed for the moment beyond the seizure of a port and a defensive perimeter. The situation on that big island was militarily peculiar. It contained powerful Japanese forces, but the Philippine guerrilla movement, here in the hands of the warlike Moros, was so strong and well led that not long after the Leyte fighting the enemy were pinned down to a few fortified areas and practically deprived of the power of movement; a considerable portion of the northern part of the island was in control of the insurgents. Elements of General R. L. Eichelberger's Eighth Army were engaged in clearing the central Philippines during March and early April against opposition that was generally weak. Now on April 17 the whole X Corps was put ashore at Cotaboto on the western face of the main mass of Mindanao. It expeditiously drove eastward through the valleys to Davao, the main Japanese center in the south, which was reached early in May. There was hard house-to-house fighting here, of the same type as at Manila, with the Japanese ultimately borne down by numbers and artillery fire.

The X Corps turned north, fanning out along several lines of communication, and simultaneously more troops were landed at Agusan in the guerrilla-held north. The Mindanao operation now took on the same character as that in Luzon—a painstaking searching out and reduction of enemy cave positions (where these did not exist the Japanese made them), whose requirements were chiefly time and ammunition.

When the operation ended there were over 317,000 Japanese dead in the Philippines and they had yielded 7,000 prisoners; the total American casualties (four fifths of them were wounded men who would recover) were 60,000. Such statistics tell more eloquently than any words the tale of a campaign in which an enemy with over-all numerical superiority was outmaneuvered and outgunned at every point through sound strategy and adroit use of the forces of air and sea.

Yet even this does not explain the complete failure of the Japanese to make any effective defense, their inability to bring anything but endurance and devotion to the business of war. The fact is that their whole military system had been based on too rigid an obedience to orders, in which there was no room for initiative on the part of commanders in the field; and on a system of "military honor" which forbade subordinates to inform their superiors that orders had not been carried out. This was neatly illustrated in the Leyte campaign. Marshal Terauchi's orders were to hold the pass at the north end of the island against the American advance while reinforcements sufficient to drive the invaders into the sea were brought through Ormoc. Neither the over-all commander at the pass nor any of his subordinates reported that post after post was falling to our attack; the commander of the reinforcing formation continued to move his transports while the American destroyers and planes were making it obviously impossible to get more than a small percentage through; and the official documents still showed the Japanese position as good, when in fact it had become desperate.

Again, all the formations in movement on the roads of Luzon when MacArthur's blow fell continued to move until they had reached their destinations and then had to be moved back again, arriving too late. Some of the Japanese local commanders knew of the attack, but their system did not allow them to act until they had received orders from above.

CHAPTER XVII

THE EUROPEAN ENEMY BREAKS

AFTER the battle lines became stabilized along the Scheldt and the frontiers of Germany in September, 1944, and the effort to outflank the enemy defensive position on the north had failed, the most important objective before the Allied High Command was the improvement of its logistic position to the point where a general assault on the Nazi defensives could be undertaken. In this question was comprehended not only the matter of bringing up supplies, which is the usual province of logistics, but also a variety of others reaching back to the sources of supply in the United States. The expenditure of artillery shells, for instance, had been far heavier than anticipated, and grave errors had been made in the War Department in ordering the types of shell needed. These errors had to be rectified, and before this was done some shortages were felt at the front during the autumn battles. The needs for replacements among combat infantry had been far underestimated, and as the Selective Service System lagged well behind the requirements in producing them, many men had to be combed out of the various specialized formations.

But the foremost necessity was that of finding new ports through which supplies already existing could be brought to the battle line. Antwerp was chosen as the best available, both because of its excellent and intact dock facilities and because its use meant a shorter haul to reach the northern end of the long fighting line where the main actions would obviously be taking place. To open Antwerp it was necessary to gain control of the islands at the mouth of the Scheldt, an operation undertaken in mid-October by Marshal Montgomery's British and Canadian forces, with a heavy attack north from the region of Antwerp and an operation in a northwesterly direction against the causeway to the island of South Beveland.

The fighting was desperate, progress was slow, and casualties were very heavy, but the island was conquered on October 30, and a campaign was then begun for the reduction of the other island, Walcheren. An attempt to flood the Germans out by cutting the dikes failed; the attack had to be undertaken as an amphibian operation which, as expected, proved costly in the extreme; nevertheless it was completed by November 9. As soon as mines were cleared from the river, ships began to use Antwerp, but the enemy retorted by opening an intensive fire of V-1 buzz-bombs against the city, which was still within easy range of the emplacements at the border. Antwerp was frightfully battered, receiving a far heavier bombardment from these weapons than London in earlier days. Liège also, as the chief communications center behind our front, was subjected to an intense fire of pilotless missiles, which caused much damage and many casualties. But the overall supply situation was eased.

MEANWHILE, the operations on the American portion of the front had become a war of position. For the whole central sector the key was the city of Metz, upon which all the roads and railroads from Lorraine and the Palatinate converge, so that its possession by the enemy gave him an effective block on movement in any direction. Early in October, 1944, a direct assault on Metz by General Patton's Third Army forces failed, and the breakdown contributed not a little to the general depression at this time. It was then decided to pinch the place out by an envelopment from both flanks at a distance beyond the range of the fortress guns.

The attack was opened on November 1 north of Nancy, as a local operation in rough ground to clear assembly areas and artillery positions from which more extensive attacks could be launched. It did not attract the attention of the Germans, who left the matter to their local reserves, and the necessary positions were gained without too severe a struggle.

The 9th Air Force, which had been set up in France to give the armies closer coöperation than could be provided by the 8th from England, now began a systematic attack on German communications throughout Lorraine. This continued for a week, more or less advertising the attack northeast of Nancy, which was opened on November 7 and immediately met by the enemy with strong counter-attacks. On the first day there was little gain against these but the Germans were much hurt by our artillery fire. On November 8 they began to yield ground and in very hard fighting were pressed back south of Metz to the ring of forts round the city itself.

November 9 saw the opening of the offensive north of the city, where the problem was to cross the swift and steep-banked Meuse. Patton made great use of armor in the early stages and won a pair of good bridgeheads on either side of Thionville, but the operation became an infantry affair when the Nazis in turn put in armor. Our tanks were not at all adapted to battle the better-armored and better-gunned German tanks, and the wooded country of Lorraine, with its narrow valleys, offered little room for the swift sweeping advances for which the American machines were intended. South of Thionville the infantry advance, with strong artillery support, broke into the ring of Metz forts on November 14 and captured some of them, finding evidence of enemy disorganization in the fact that few were properly supplied with ammunition and some did not have all their guns in position.

The next day the Germans tried an amored counterattack with a whole panzer division, but the attack had been anticipated and was completely broken up. This really sealed the fate of the great fortress. So many of its supporting roads were now either in our hands or under our fire that a break anywhere in the line would cut it off. The Germans retreated along the whole front to approximately the line of the frontier, where mountain ridges with their own newer and better-designed fortifications gave them superior positions for defense. Some of the Metz forts continued to hold out with small garrisons till mid-December; after that the place became an American communications center.

Farther north the great sweep of the summer had carried through Belgium and Luxembourg with hardly a check till it reached the German frontier. Here our First Army (Hodges) was in position next to the Third, with the Ninth (Simpson) being gradually built into the line between it and the British, all facing east along the Belgian border. These constituted the Twelfth Army group, under Bradley's command. The key of the line at this point was the city of Aachen, a road center like Metz, and of paramount importance because through it lay the only routes by which the German plains could be reached without campaigning through ridge after ridge of fortified hills as in the south, or reaches of inundated flats, as farther north. The objective was the plain leading to Cologne; secondarily, the mining district of the Saar.

American forces reached the place on September 3 and got into the outer edge of Aachen but could make no further progress and were driven out by a German rally. Although small territorial gains were made, attempts at encirclement north and south of the town broke down in heavy fighting during early October, as did a direct attack after an aerial bombardment rivaling that of Cassino. Antwerp was not yet open at this date and the enemy could reinforce more rapidly than we could. They showed no hesitation in using their tactically superior armor, and in the stone-built town the air bombs only created rubble heaps which the more effectively protected cellar positions where the defenders were dug in around their guns. There was an organizational pause while fresh units of the Ninth Army were moved into position. Then General Hodges began the systematic reduction of each strong point in turn, using, principally, self-propelled guns protected against return fire by a host of other batteries. The operations north and south of Aachen put our artillery in position to cut off supply and reinforcement, and on October 21 Aachen surrendered.

Some distance to the east, the small river Roer courses through a double line of hills in a direction mainly northward, but beyond these hills a fairly open plain extends to Cologne and the banks of the Rhine. The hills and the towns along the Roer had been worked into the Siegfried defensive system. Their long stand in Aachen had given the Germans opportunity to move in new artillery and to improve these positions in the light of experience, an opportunity which they did not neglect. Their general method was to provide a wide variety of concreted gun positions with protected approaches and to move self-propelled artillery into each in turn for a few salvos, withdrawing before counteraction could be taken. The weather had now become so very unfavorable that air operations were severely limited. The Antwerp supply line was not yet in efficient operation. Nevertheless General Eisenhower decided on a winter campaign against this flank of the enemy defenses.

He had several reasons for this decision. One was that the Nazis were evidently in grave difficulties about reserves. They had instituted a combing-out process in home industry, converted many lines-of-communication troops into fighting units, and enlisted a vast "peoples' army" to make good the losses they had suffered in France and on the Russian front. But all these new units required training, and, if they could be forced into open field operations before this training was complete, we would have every advantage. Another reason was the known unwillingness of the Germans to conduct winter campaigns, together with the fact that the Russian front had been quiescent since September. If the Nazis could be forced to fight all winter they would have to meet a massive Soviet spring offensive with men exhausted by warfare under the hardest conditions, instead of with units that would ordinarily have spent several months in rest areas. Finally, ground existed for believing that the German scientists were near success with weapons far more deadly than V-1 or V-2, and there was at least a chance that one of these might succeed in changing the whole face of the war unless the Germans could first be defeated in the field.

I⊤ had been many years since northern Europe experienced a winter so unfavorable to military operations as that encountered by our troops when they began their offensive on November 1, 1944; icy rains, freezing mud, and low clouds kept our air forces grounded for most of the day and interfered with artillery observation. The warfare was strictly one of positions. The British attacked in the north to clear whatever pockets the Germans still had west of the Maas and to support the left flank of the direct frontal assault undertaken by the Ninth and First armies together. In Lorraine the Third and Seventh armies edged forward slowly to keep the Germans from moving reserves. It was dogged and extremely hard fighting. Gains were limited to a few hundred yards a day and frequently were canceled by counterattacks. The capture of each stone village or pillbox became a separate operation; all fighting was on a purely tactical level. The favorable features were that the Germans were forced to commit reserves they would have preferred to withhold; and as some of these reserves were very green formations with only six weeks of training, and as our aerial attacks on their communications kept up unremittingly, their casualties were far higher than ours.

Early in December the banks of the Roer were reached at two or three points, and now a new difficulty appeared. There was a system of dams at the headwaters of that stream. If the sluices were suddenly opened the resulting flash flood would be fatal to any attempt to cross the stream. While an effort was undertaken to reduce the bridgehead on the west bank which the Germans still held at Düren, another offensive was undertaken in a southeasterly direction into the wild country between Monschau and Schmidt to obtain possession of the dams. This was gaining slowly when an entirely new factor entered the campaign.

After the signal defeats in France, Hitler had restored Marshal Rundstedt to the command of his armies in the west. Their success in holding our forces at the frontier owed much to his organizing and strategic ability. Early in December, under direct orders from Hitler, he began preparing the first winter offensive undertaken by a German army since Frederick the Great.

By such devices as stripping the garrisons of Norway and Czechoslovakia, a force of 24 divisions, mostly below full strength, was assembled opposite the frontier of Luxembourg and that part of Belgium which adjoins it on the north. German communications in this area were none too good, but those on our side of the line were very bad indeed, for here lies the rugged region of the Ardennes, now deep in snow. We could not quickly reinforce against an attack. Once a German advance crossed this region it would reach Liège, the main communication center for all the armies in the north, with Givet and Dinant on the Meuse where, as the Germans knew, we had vast stores of fuel, food, and ammunition. If these points were reached, the drive would become self-sustaining. The attackers fully counted on its doing so and at least reaching Antwerp with the resultant cutting off of all the Allied armies in the north. Thus, as the Germans moved forward to the attack on December 16, their propagandists shouted that they would be back in Paris by Christmas.

They very nearly made it. So many of the First

Army's troops had been drawn into the fighting along the Roer that a great part of the front opposite the attack was held by a new division without battle experience, the 106th. It was cut to pieces in the first rush. Our High Command had noted the German concentration, but had estimated that it was intended for counterattack against the flanks of our own movement toward Cologne, since it consisted mainly of infantry, our intelligence having failed to note the presence of two fresh and strong armored divisions brought in from Norway. The enemy used parachutists in great numbers, many of them in American uniforms, against our lines of communication. Heavy fogs protected them from our air forces. In three days the attack had gone 20 miles into our lines and had taken prisoners equal to the strength of a division. Communications were disorganized throughout the whole Ardennes triangle.

General Eisenhower reacted with speed and vigor. A corps was drawn from the British to hold Liège and the northern part of the line of the Meuse. The American First Army as well as the Ninth were placed under Montgomery's command since he could more conveniently control their movements from the north side of the break, and he vigorously counterattacked that shoulder of the penetration. General Bradley took over control of the group of armies on the south flank. He ordered up the 101st Airborne Division, which had been in reserve, to hold Bastogne, road center for all the middle Ardennes, while the Seventh Army slid leftward to take over the front of the Third. Patton brought that force up to attack the south flank of the bulge at a speed rarely seen in war; his 5th Division moved 69 miles in a day and was in action by nightfall.

The key of the battle proved to be Bastogne. The 101st had barely arrived before it was surrounded, and though joined by retreating elements of the 10th Armored Division, it was so thoroughly cut off that it had to be supplied by air for a week. During that week it was attacked all around the perimeter of its position day and night. The defense was heroic to the last degree. When the Germans sent in a flag of truce requesting surrender, and accompanied it with maps to show that the position of the defenders was hopeless, they were met with the simple reply "Nuts!" from Brigadier-General A. C. McAuliffe. The phrase is likely to endure long in American memory.

Lacking the roads thus denied them, the Germans had to swing a circuit northward, and being stopped by the British in their progress toward Liège had to make another swing southward in the direction of our supply depots. On the 22nd the weather cleared; the whole of our tactical air forces were thrown onto their supply columns and

armored forces moving through the narrow channels of the mountains, and as these convoys were
numerous, the destruction was great. By the 25th
Patton's armored formations were making their
presence so much felt that Rundstedt had to detail
many of his troops for defensive duties. All the fire
went out of his drive and on the next day besieged
Bastogne was relieved.

Now the problem for the enemy became one of
getting his men out of the most forward areas of advance while under constant attack and with all the
roads leading from the area heavily shelled. He
retreated in good order and so slowly that it was
the end of January before he was back across the
frontier. But the problem was never really solved,
for in the course of the battle he lost 110,000 prisoners and another 110,000 casualties of other types,
along with the full mechanical equipment of two
armored armies.

This was the end of the German strategic reserve.
When the Russians launched a prodigious attack all
along the eastern front on January 22, there were
no reinforcements to send against them. The whole
front began rolling back; and though the Nazis had
anticipated the attack, they were by no means prepared for the facts that it was made in greater force
than any other offensive of the war and was backed
by transportation equipment that made demolitions of no effect. A month from the beginning of

the movement it was on the Oder, threatening Stettin, Dresden, and even Berlin. General Eisenhower could prepare his own spring offensive in the full confidence that if he achieved a break-through anywhere, he would go all the way.

On the Lorraine front the Germans had launched covering attacks in support of their Ardennes drive of December, 1944, but the men of the Seventh Army merely pulled out of the advanced positions that had been held by the Third and retired to the old fortifications of the Maginot Line. On these the Germans failed to make any impression. Still farther south, the French in Alsace had worked through the Belfort Gap into the plain during the fall. As winter came on, they operated an encirclement with the help of the Seventh Army units coming down from the north, cut off a number of German formations, and by the end of January had cleared the whole left bank of the Rhine. General Eisenhower held this long stretch with relatively light forces, concentrating toward his strategic left, while General Patton's Third Army gradually worked down to take over part of the positions it had previously held along the borders of the Palatinate.

These preliminary moves, with preparations behind the lines, occupied most of February, 1945. On the 9th of that month the Canadians on the north started another flank-clearing operation in the region where the Rhine makes its westward bend. Each army down the line was to swing into the attack in succession, with Simpson's American Ninth making the main effort, straight across the Roer toward Düsseldorf. Floods delayed the Ninth's movement, the Germans concentrated against the Canadians and stopped them after some initial gains. It was Rundstedt's last success and used his last reserves. When the Ninth did attack on the moonlit night of February 23 under cover of chemical smokes, it broke right through with surprising ease. Half a dozen bridgeheads were established before dawn, before noon bridges were up and armor was crossing them, striking into the rear areas of the troops opposing the Canadians and for the Rhine bridges across which these troops were supported.

Swarms of Allied planes covered the advance. The Germans could make no head against them, their communications began to go, and on the night of March 1 their High Command ordered withdrawal from this whole northern salient down to the mountains that enclose the Meuse. The retreating forces blew all the Rhine bridges as they retired and fought well during the movement; but there was no time for the elaborate mining and demolitions which had covered similar retreats in Africa and Italy, and great numbers of the enemy were cut off and captured by our armor in the open plains.

Still more prisoners were taken when the Ninth began to fan southward toward Cologne while Hodges' First attacked on its part of the front. All the stone villages had been converted into fortresses, but the Nazis were now badly outnumbered and the mobility of our forces was such as to increase the effect of their numbers. When a knot of resistance was encountered, planes, tanks, and self-propelled guns appeared within the hour to lay down an unbearable concentration of fire. Cologne, a ruined city, fell on March 7.

At Bonn the enemy tried to hold, in order to let some of their troops from the southern part of the front reach the Rhine, but on that same March 7 the 9th Armored Division broke through loose German lines to reach the river at Remagen south of Bonn. One of the great bridges stands there. The 9th found it damaged by Allied aerial bombs and mined for demolition, but still standing, and defended by only a handful of infantry who were driven off before they could blow the bridge. The 9th crossed at once, and on the opposite bank began to spread out and dig in. They were counterattacked that day only by weak infantry formations. During the night the German area commander got some artillery together and next morning attacked again, energetically shelling both the bridge itself and the American position, from a chain of hills east of the river. But by this time the bridgehead was increasing rapidly both in strength and extent, for General Hodges had at once recognized the importance of this foothold beyond a stream which is one of the toughest military obstacles of the world, and had called off every other operation to pour reinforcements in behind the 9th Armored.

As both sides brought up troops a major battle developed, the Allied planes maintaining a continuous patrol over the bridge and German planes constantly trying to break through to bomb. An attack on March 11 captured most of the German observation posts in the dominating hills but could not be driven much deeper. On the other hand our forces made steady progress in extending the bridgehead along the flanks, where our artillery fire could take their positions in enfilade from the west bank. On the 17th the bridge collapsed, but by that date there were already three pontoon bridges in support and two more were shortly added, over which the whole First Army poured into an area that was now fifteen miles long by eight miles deep.

But by this date the truly fatal blow had been struck. From the Rhine at a point just south of Remagen runs the jagged range of the Eiffel Mountains, cut by few and easily defensible passes to the north. This chain formed the northern defense of the Palatinate, which on its west and south was

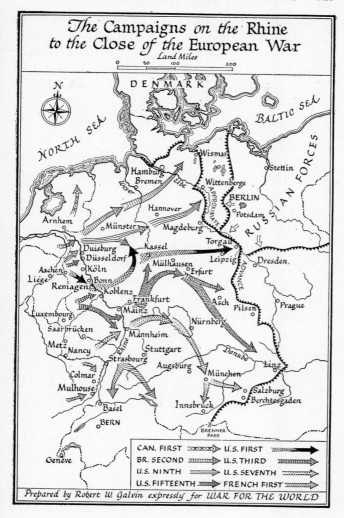

The Campaigns on the Rhine
to the Close of the European War

Land Miles
0   50   100   200

Prepared by Robert W. Galvin expressly for WAR FOR THE WORLD

CAN. FIRST   U.S. FIRST
BR. SECOND   U.S. THIRD
U.S. NINTH   U.S. SEVENTH
U.S. FIFTEENTH   FRENCH FIRST

covered by the Siegfried fortifications. The main line of communication is by the Moselle Valley from Coblenz to Trier. Against the southern face of this huge triangle, Patch's Seventh Army had been working through obstacles since the beginning of the offensive, and had not been making much progress. Patton's Third Army attacked in the region of Prüm on the north and at Trier, trying to pinch out the latter town. It seemed obvious to the German command that he intended to work down the valley of the Moselle, and the enemy shifted many of their troops in that direction, counterattacking vigorously and holding the American advance after Trier fell on March 2.

They misread the American commander's intention. As soon as the Germans had committed themselves to the Trier counterattack, Patton put the 4th Armored Division into the Prüm area in an attack on a very narrow front along the steep southward slopes of the Eiffel range. It broke right through with scarcely a casualty, going over thirty miles in a day, and was immediately followed by another armored division and several of infantry. On March 7 it struck the Rhine near Coblenz and turned south, with more armor and mechanized infantry coming along behind. The Moselle Valley communication line of the Germans fighting far to the west was cut; Patton's spearhead, meeting only weak and ineffective resistance, pressed on past the mouth of that stream, which was crossed on March 14. Three days later both Worms and Mainz were taken and the 4th Armored rushed on up the bank of the Rhine to cut the communications of the whole group of armies in the Palatinate.

These had begun to retreat when Coblenz fell, for the German command had so concentrated on holding its fortified frontiers that there was nothing within the rear areas to halt Patton's rush. The retreating troops were now vigorously attacked both by the Third Army along the Moselle Valley and from the south by the Seventh, which in the intervening weeks had worked through most of the vast minefields. General Patch of the Seventh threw his armor into the pursuit, and now the fast, long-range American tanks were as far superior to German armor as the latter had been superior in close fighting. The Nazi formations could only escape by leaving larger and larger proportions of their numbers as self-sacrificing rear guards, and, even so, not 10 percent of the men in all that group of armies got away across the Rhine.

At Allied Headquarters the passage of the Rhine had loomed as an operation quite equal in difficulty to the landing in Normandy. Elaborate preparations for it had been made, especially in the north, where Marshal Montgomery, with the British and Canadian forces and the American Ninth Army, was facing the great industrial district of the Ruhr, where the bulk of the defenders had been concentrated. On the evening of March 23, 1945, the crossing was simultaneously begun by the Second British and American Ninth armies, two airborne divisions being dropped ahead of the line of attack. The effort was everywhere successful and the two armies advanced abreast against opposition that was often tenacious but could find little good ground for defense in an area where Allied mechanization, ably seconded from the air, gave our forces such extreme mobility.

In the meantime the Third Army elements had seized two more crossings at Mainz and Oppenheim, and on March 22 Patton began sending his formations across, driving straight east against opposition everywhere weak. The armies that should have defended this area had been destroyed in the Palatinate, and though Hitler called every German to arms in defense of the fatherland and found weapons for a good many, he could not provide them with military organization or training. How far the disintegration of the once-great Nazi armies had progressed was made clear when Hodges of the First Army delivered a general attack from the Remagen bridgehead. At the north end of the bridgehead area a small river, the Sieg, flows into the Rhine from the east at right angles between steep hills. During the previous two weeks Hodges' men had made several probing attacks against this river line and the Germans shifted a portion of their Ruhr forces southward to hold it. On March 25 the First attacked in force, but to the surprise of the enemy, in a southeasterly direction, right away from the Sieg line. They broke through easily, flung one column off southward to capture Frankfurt, then drove straight east and north in a wide sweep outside the whole Ruhr area, the general direction being Kassel-Paderborn.

The Third Army joined in this great wheel, parallel with but outside the orbit of the First. The Seventh, which had by now forced its own crossings, drove east and southeast to cut the roads to the Bavarian highlands, where it was thought that the fanatic remnants of the Nazis might attempt to stand. Wherever these had leaders and supplies they did fight on, notably in the Ruhr, which had to be reduced piece by piece through the attacks of the First and the Ninth, and the new Fifteenth Army. But throughout April the operation of cutting Germany up into parts went on virtually unchecked, while the Russians were winning Berlin, house by house. On the 9th of that month the Allied forces in Italy made a general assault on the positions that had held there so long, and this attack too swept everything before it. The whole German structure was now in a state of collapse; resistance in most cases became merely formal, and after

Hitler committed suicide in the blazing ruins of Berlin an emergency government gave its unconditional surrender to the Allies on May 7, 1945.

To its own people this government explained that their country had been overborne by an accumulation of mechanical weapons. This was untrue. The Germans had been beaten because on the sea they could find no means of preventing our troops from reaching Europe; because in the air they could find none of keeping our bombers from pounding their transportation system to pieces and cutting off their sources of fuel; and, above all, because on land they could find no officers who used the means at hand as well as ours, whatever those means might be.

CHAPTER XVIII

THE END OF JAPAN

THE first B-29 raid from Saipan against Japan was
flown on November 24, 1944, and was rapidly followed by others. The results were somewhat dis-
appointing. The quality of information from within
the beleaguered country was not all that could be
desired, but it was clear from photo-reconnaissance
that, in comparison to the effort and materials expended, the damage was comparatively slight. In
the meantime, as soon as the organizational period
of the new base was complete, the Army Air Force
had sent one of its best young operational officers,
Major-General Curtis LeMay, to take charge. He
reached the conclusion that even with the accurate
bombsight it was difficult to obtain sufficient hits
on targets that were usually small and always well
distributed. As a result he sent the big bombers in
at levels under 10,000 feet in a trial raid late in
December. This time the results were thoroughly
satisfactory; nor were the losses at the lower level
of bombing such as to discourage the operation.

But as time and the bombing program went on,

two flaws appeared. The first was that at these lower levels the big planes suffered damage from both anti-aircraft fire and the attentions of Japanese fighters. The damage was not sufficient to bring many of them down at once, but a number of the expensive machines were lost in forced landings at sea. Submarines of the American fleet worked out an admirable rescue service, picking up more than 500 men. But still the loss in planes was serious. The second difficulty lay in the Japanese reaction to the bombing program. They sent down medium bombers of their own from the Bonins to make suicidal crash landings among the planes parked on the Marianas fields, and though many of these bombers were shot down before reaching their destination, enough attained it to make the counterattack a matter of concern. Nor did repeated air strikes on the Bonins fields appreciably reduce this activity.

The navy's own strategic program was still for the capture of some of the Ryukyus, but for the moment the support of the B-29 program became more important. As soon as General MacArthur's Luzon operation had been placed on a self-sustaining basis, therefore, the fleet hurried north to carry through preparations which had already been made for attacking Iwo Jima in the Volcano Islands, the southern extension of the Bonin group. Iwo Jima lies 750 miles from Tokyo. Long-range fighters from it could cover the B-29s on their flights, and other fighters could eliminate enemy counterattacks at their inception; moreover, it would afford a way station for crippled planes.

The ships were now once more under the command of Admiral Spruance, with Admiral Mitscher in charge of the carriers. The troops for the operation were three divisions of Marines (3rd, 4th, and 5th) commanded by Major-General Harry Schmidt, who had led the ground forces on Saipan. The island has a deep coating of sifting ash. A tall volcano rises at its southern end and at the northern end a long slope leads up to a high plateau from which another volcano rises. There were only two practicable beaches, both so well commanded by the elevated positions that a surprise landing would be impossible. Therefore, the attack had to be a straight frontal one, at a place where the enemy expected it, and nothing would serve but overwhelming force applied with the greatest energy.

This application began on February 16, 1945, a year to the day from the first attack on Truk. The fast carriers ran close up to Japan for a strike at Tokyo and the plane factories and airfields around it. There was heavy aerial fighting; we lost 49 planes and the enemy 322, besides numbers destroyed on the ground. Meanwhile the battleships had moved in against Iwo, which they subjected

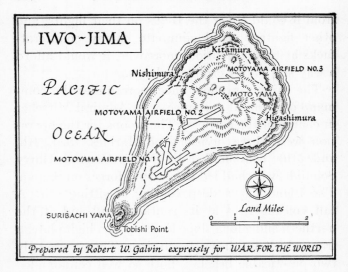

IWO~JIMA

PACIFIC

OCEAN

Kitamura

Nishimura

MOTOYAMA AIRFIELD NO.3

MOTO YAMA

MOTOYAMA AIRFIELD NO. 2

Higashimura

MOTOYAMA AIRFIELD NO 1

N

SURIBACHI YAMA

Tobishi Point

Land Miles

0   ½   1   2

Prepared by Robert W. Galvin expressly for WAR FOR THE WORLD

to a shelling more intense than those at Kwajalein or Peleliu, combing over every inch of it for days. Escort carriers added a bomb attack; so did army planes working from Saipan, and the fast carrier force on its return from the Tokyo strike. At dawn on February 19, landings began, with the 4th and 5th Marine Divisions going in.

They met some mortar fire as they approached the beach and a couple of LSTs were hit, but this first stage was crossed with comparative ease. But as the Marines attempted to advance from their beach the true strength and nature of the defenses became manifest. The beach itself was almost knee-deep in the gritty volcanic ash which clogged the tracks of tanks and offered no concealment whatever. Under this ash the whole island was honeycombed with an elaborate system of caves, tunnels, and pillboxes, so deep they had hardly been touched at all by that furious preliminary bombardment. From every one of these the Japanese opened fire with weapons of all descriptions; from the plateau on the north, from Mt. Suribachi on the south, came the shells of big guns and a new, very formidable type of rocket.

Once more it was touch and go, with some possibility that the landing could not be made good. Supplies could not be landed nor the wounded evacuated; there was no artillery ashore. The Marines clung doggedly to their ground, working forward to knock out pillbox after pillbox at close range. They had one advantage seldom found in previous landings, in that the island was small with deep water close inshore. Destroyers of the fleet moved in and, aided by new fire-control methods, laid shells with pinpoint accuracy as little as twenty yards ahead of the advancing troops. They were seldom able to smash the heavily concreted pillboxes, but their fire kept the defenders under cover while the Marines crept forward with demolition charges—normally losing several of their number by fire from flanking pillboxes in the process.

In this manner the attackers fought their way across the narrow neck of the island, on the first

night. During that night the Japanese came out
of their holes in a heavy counterattack, which was
beaten off under the constant glare of star shells,
and in the morning the slow advance began again.
It was February 23 before Mt. Suribachi had been
stormed and some relief obtained from the plung-
ing mortar fire that had caused so many casualties.
Amphibian tanks got ashore after this; two days
later the attackers were fighting in the main village
toward the north end of the island and clearing
out a system of more than 100 interconnected
caves, each 30 to 40 feet deep. It was well into
March before the last fighting was done. When it
was over, 20,000 Japanese were dead and the
Marines had had the bloodiest battle of their history, with 20,196 casualties of their own. Offshore
the fleet was under constant attack from Kamikaze
which sank one escort carrier and inflicted terrific
injuries on two of the large carriers.

But even before the island was entirely won,
bulldozers were at work improving the airfields
for the use of our fighters, and on March 9 the great
fleet of B-29s with full fighter escort struck Tokyo.
They carried nothing but fire bombs, which they
spread broadcast across a section of the city where
small airplane parts were manufactured in the
homes. A wind fanned the flames; all measures of
protection proved futile and over a third of the
Japanese capital burned to the ground.

The way was now clear for the attack on the Ryukyus. It was directed at Okinawa, the largest of the group, only 370 miles from Kyushu, 65 miles long and irregular in shape, with a rugged and wooded northern portion, the southern half well populated, but much cut up by ravines. Preliminary estimates were that some 80,000 Japanese troops held the place. To overcome them the new Tenth Army was detailed under Lieutenant-General S. B. Buckner; it consisted of a corps of Marines and one composed of three divisions of army troops (27th, 77th, and 96th) that had frequently worked with the Navy. The whole fleet was in support, together with a powerful squadron of British ships.

Offshore from the southern tip of Okinawa are some small islands, the Kerama Retto. These afford a fairly well-sheltered anchorage against the typhoons that are very frequent in that part of the world. They were attacked on March 26, 1945, while mine sweepers of the fleet were working off Okinawa itself. By March 31 they were in our hands, and a vast fleet of supply ships and repair vessels moved in, in preparation for the landing on Okinawa's western shore the next morning. The landing was accomplished readily and with little loss, the army getting 50,000 men ashore by evening of the first day and holding a beachhead two miles in depth. The drive was across the island's narrow waist; by April 4 the opposite shore had been reached, and the Marines turned north against the wooded ground, where the Japanese were expected to be found in force among the hills, while the army men swung south against the populated section and its formal defenses.

But by April 4, also, the campaign had developed a feature new to the Pacific war. Japanese planes, generally in small groups, had attacked our mine sweepers and their covering vessels off Okinawa. This was anticipated; the novelty lay in the fact that nearly all these attacks were by Kamikaze, the suicide planes, which succeeded in sinking a couple of the mine sweepers. Among the Kerama Retto Islands were found a number of small fast boats heavily charged with explosives, obviously designed to be used as suicide craft. It began to look as though the Japanese boasts of converting their entire air force into a Kamikaze corps were not far short of the fact.

These fanatics had been gathering on the Kyushu airfields and it was of the utmost importance to keep them from getting in among the transports and supply vessels off Okinawa. Admiral Spruance took the fleet north for a series of carrier strikes, while Admiral Frazer ran south with the British fleet for a similar attack on the Shikishima islands.

The dual move provoked a remarkable battle. The Japanese had planned a massive Kamikaze

strike against our fleet while their own should
run down the East China Sea to attack the Okinawa beachhead. The American carrier strike came
on them a little too soon for their plan. Several
hundred planes were destroyed on the Kyushu airfields and the fleet that was to attack our Okinawa
beachhead was reduced to the new battleship
Yamato, a light cruiser, and ten destroyers, which
nevertheless began the run down the East China
Sea.

It was spotted, and on April 7 Admiral Mitscher
flew off the fleet's planes in a massive strike. All
day they hammered at the enemy ships; *Yamato*,
the cruiser and four of the destroyers went down,
and three more of the destroyers were crippled.
But at the same time the enemy attacked our fleet
with a swarm of nearly 600 Kamikaze. Several of
our light craft were damaged or sunk and one big
carrier badly mauled. Four days later, with the
fleet still off Kyushu, came another wave of Kamikaze and again there was damage.

On April 12 the Japs shifted their attack to the
transports off Okinawa beachhead, bringing in a
new type of suicide plane in addition to the others
—the Baka, a rocket-propelled, and manned, aerial
torpedo, which was carried by a larger plane and
released near its destination. Our patrol shot down
151 Japanese that day; and on our return to Kyushu on April 15–16, in another air battle of the

same type, 249 more were destroyed. But on both occasions some of our ships were hit and the impact of the bomb-loaded planes always resulted in frightful damage and heavy casualties.

THE situation caused concern, for although few ships were sunk, and those all among the lighter types, many of the big carriers had to go in for repairs. The strength of the fleet was being steadily cut down, while the ground battle on Okinawa seemed endless. The light resistance our forces had encountered after landing on April 1, 1945, proved to be only the first phase of a new type of defense.

At the north end of the island the Marines encountered only moderate opposition and by the middle of April had cleared the rough ground there except for mopping-up operations. In the south, after a rapid early advance, the army troops ran into a system of fortifications that verged on the fantastic. The ground was cut up by ravines sheltering some natural limestone caves; these had been added to and built up with tunnels until the whole island was almost as much of a network as the much smaller Iwo Jima. This setup was familiar, but the Japanese had added the new feature of quantities of artillery, including mortars of a new type and of gigantic size, which permitted the defenders of the caves to take far more aggressive action than had been encountered elsewhere.

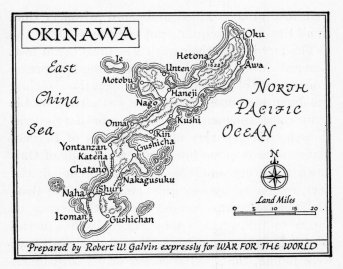

OKINAWA

East
China
Sea

Oku
Hetona
Ie
Unten
Awa
Motobu
Haneji
Nago
Onna
Kushi
Yontanzan
Kin
Gushicha
Katena
Chatano
Nakagusuku
Naha
Shuri
Itoman
Gushichan

NORTH
PACIFIC
OCEAN

N

Land Miles
0 5 10 15 20

Prepared by Robert W. Galvin expressly for WAR FOR THE WORLD

The number of their troops also proved to be a considerable underestimate, and they did not hesitate to use these troops in almost continual suicidal night counterattacks, one of which nearly drove the 27th Division into the sea. The whole campaign evolved into an exhausting form of siege warfare, in which each individual Japanese position had to be taken by hand as on Iwo Jima. The divisions were rotated in action, and the Marine Corps was brought down from the north to help out the army. Inch by inch progress was made until June 21, when organized resistance ended. The island had cost us 39,000 casualties ashore, plus another 10,000 in the fleet offshore. The Japanese lost 110,000 killed and more prisoners than in all the other conquests put together—7,800.

The fact is that their spirit was breaking at last. General MacArthur had been named Supreme Commander of ground forces for operations against the Japanese home islands. He was setting up his army commands and conducting subsidiary operations for the recovery of the oil ports of Borneo; planes were flooding into the new airfields of Okinawa till every available inch was occupied; the fleet, reinforced by new units and a powerful British squadron, was running up to the coasts of Japan to throw shells into Tokyo itself and the steel mills along the shore. While all these blows were falling, the fanatic leaders who had planned the conquest of half a world were making a series of discoveries. The Okinawa campaign had caused concern in the American command, but it had really been the last gasp of the Japanese air force; they lost over 3,400 planes and their replacement capacity was now so seriously impaired that the Japanese High Command was forced to order the remaining machines withheld for defense against the invasion of Japan. Even for the remaining planes, there was a serious shortage of gasoline, and the capture of Okinawa had placed·our ships and planes in position from which they cut off any further supply of the natural product.

Many of the best formations of the Japanese

army had been destroyed among the islands or were now cut off in the south. In fact, the spring of 1945 saw a general movement of Japanese troops from the newly won lands in southern China up toward Manchuria and the coasts of the Sea of Japan. That area was the home of the army that had started the nation on its career of aggression. There it expected to make a stand even after the loss of the home islands, with some idea of wearing out our patience. This hope vanished on August 8 when the Soviet Government declared war and sent its powerful, battle-experienced forces through the passes into Manchuria. But two days before that, on August 6, there had already occurred an event which threw the Russian attack into the shade.

A B-29 of the strategic air force passed over the city of Hiroshima and dropped a single bomb in which the energy of the atom was released. Since the beginning of the war, British, Canadian, and American scientists had been working on the problem of harnessing that energy. So had the Germans, and the fear that they might attain the goal first had been one of the reasons for General Eisenhower's hurry in the early spring of 1945. Now it had been found, and the results were all that imagination predicted. Hiroshima, previously undamaged, was completely destroyed and something like 80,000 people were killed. Three days later another

The Position Versus Japan

Prepared by Robert W. Galvin expressly for WAR FOR THE WORLD

atomic bomb similarly pulverized most of the great port city of Nagasaki and on August 14, 1945, the Japanese government capitulated.

As the Germans had done, the Japanese explained their surrender on the basis of the mechanical odds—the atomic bomb. But we have ample evidence that even before the first bomb was dropped the leaders of the empire had already decided that it was useless to continue a struggle in which all operations were reduced to a suicidal passive defense. This had been accomplished by the ability of our now unchallengeable navy to transmit to any point overwhelming forces of soldiers who, through their mobility and command of the air, were always superior to the enemy in ground operations.

By their own reports after the war, neither the Japanese nor the German enemy was particularly impressed by the performance of these soldiers as infantry. Our men lacked the fanaticism of the former and the exquisite skill which the latter had acquired through years of devotion to no other business but that of war. Yet the casualties of the American infantry service were high—perhaps exceptionally high—being nearly half of the 1,200,-000 casualties our armed forces suffered during the conflict. Out of a total of eleven million men borne on the rolls in army and navy together, this indicates sufficient courage and devotion for the purpose. The fact is that neither the Germans (though they had spent years in working out the science of war) nor the Japanese (who had begun consciously to prepare for the conflict as early as 1927) realized the implications for modern war that modern technology and modern methods possessed: the fact that the infantry soldier was no longer the arbiter of the battlefield nor the brave and capable seaman of the naval action.

The Germans, who affected so little concern about our infantry, were indignant about American artillery and planes, which struck them down without an opportunity for reply. They protested bitterly that the fight was never "fair"; that in every action our superior transportation equipment gave us the advantage of numbers. The Japanese naval commander in the notable instance of the Battle of Empress Augusta Bay (November 1, 1943) withdrew from the action because he was being repeatedly hit by enemies he could not even see (his own radar did not work) and of whose force he could form no estimate. Over both Germans and Japanese the victory for our side was technological.

This does not in the least detract from the courage of the men who handled the weapons. World War II was so vast that individual acts of heroism became insignificant, yet no war in which Americans had been engaged produced more of them, not in absolute terms alone, but in proportion to the numbers engaged. No war produced so few instances of panic or cowardice, whether in relative or absolute numbers. This fact is perhaps related to the other fact that for the first time since 1861 our dearest ideals and ideas were engaged. Nor does the technological side of the triumph detract from the intelligence of our leaders. Rather it increases the respect one must feel for them, as the leaders of the American Revolution are respected because they used correctly the American riflemen fighting from under cover.

But it is important for us to recognize that the victory was technological, not on the battlefield alone. This technology brought something new to the whole science and art of war, and indeed to that of human collaboration for the achievement of a great purpose; it was the specific American contribution to the general victory. The British made an immense contribution to that victory; for a whole year they held back the European Axis, armed with the strength and industry of a continent, and they had resiliency enough at the close of that ordeal to win one of the few absolutely decisive victories of the whole conflict. The Russians contributed enormously; it was they who contained, dispersed, and finally broke the backs of those German armies who had run unchecked from the Vistula to the Pyrenees and the Nile. They paid for it with seven million casualties as against our million.

Yet both of these contributions, quantitatively huge, were made within the old frames of reference, within the bounds of the old art of war, in which strategy, tactics, and courage are the determining factors.

What America introduced was a new art of war in which logistics usurped many of the functions of the other branches—the thing the Nazis referred to as "total war" but never quite understood or found the means to put into practice. This may be demonstrated statistically. It is an old truism of naval war that, unless a conflict becomes very lengthy indeed, the number of ships with which a combatant begins the war are in the main those with which he ends it, very small craft excepted. In World War II this remained true for the British navy, the German, the Japanese, and the Italian. The American navy began the war with a force of something over 300 combatant ships. At the close it possessed 1,167 major warships and only a single vessel of the pre-war fleet was still of sufficient first-line efficiency to participate in the final attacks on Japan. A program for building over 80,000 landing craft had been undertaken and nearly 60,000 of them had been built. All the combatants made some use of women in uniform for various rear area services; the American Wacs,

Waves, and Spars outnumbered all the rest of the women's services put together.

In this new art of war it was unimportant that we brought to the field only 100 combat divisions against 125 Japanese and nearly 100 German (the remainder of their divisions were pinned down and largely destroyed by the Russians). The important factor was that with the aid of the British, on land and sea, the Allied forces possessed a continual superiority of fire power at every important point of contact. It was in this domain of coöperation all the way back to the factories that the American contribution lay. The Germans and Japanese regarded infantry fighting as the index and critical factor in war; the American contribution was to make it one element in a vast complex, here for the first time successfully integrated.

BIBLIOGRAPHICAL NOTE

For a variety of reasons the naval side of World War II has been much more adequately documented than operations on land. Probably the best brief general history is Shugg and De Weerd's *World War II, A Concise History;* but it suffers from some inaccuracies in the treatment of the naval war and from the authors' anxiety to mention everything, so that a sense of proportion is lost. An excellent running account of the war will be found in the current files of the *Field Artillery Journal,* though this also is affected by the myopia inevitably attendant upon the writing about events which are still in progress.

The official reports of the leaders in the war, compiled soon after it was over, are of the greatest value, and those of General Marshall and Marshal Montgomery are written with a skill which would make them interesting reading matter regardless of subject. General Marshall's report is titled *The Winning of the War in Europe and the Pacific;* Marshal Montgomery's, *Operations in North-West Europe. The Report of the U. S. Army Air Forces* by General H. H. Arnold, the *Reports to the Secretary of the Navy* by Admiral Ernest J. King, and *Eisenhower's Own Story of the War* belong in the same category. Much material on American as well as British aviation forces is contained in *Bomber Offensive* by Marshal of the R. A. F. Sir Arthur Harris.

In some details, particularly with reference to the strategic concepts, it is difficult to reconcile Marshal Montgomery's account with those of Eisenhower and Marshall. The reader will find Captain Harry C. Butcher's *My Three Years with Eisenhower* useful. Lt. Col. A. H. Burne's *Strategy as Exemplified in the Second World War* offers illuminating comment. Ralph Ingersoll's *Top Secret* is violent, controversial, and often demonstrably inaccurate, but it contains some useful detail on the European campaigns. A useful corrective is supplied by Major-General Sir Francis de Guingand's *Operation Victory.* The U. S. Army Historical Section has published and is continuing to publish a long series of studies on individual operations. They are somewhat uneven in character but the best are very good indeed; those on *Omaha Beachhead, St. Lô,* and the *Volturno* deserve special mention.

Two quasi-official publications head the list on the naval war. As this is written only two volumes of Professor S. E. Morison's *History of U. S. Naval Operations in World War II* have appeared; the list is to be extended to fourteen. Captain Walter Karig, with various collaborators, has produced three volumes of his *Battle Report.* This work presents a more humanized picture of events, but the first two volumes, dealing with the operations from Pearl Harbor to Coral Sea and the war in the Atlantic, were written while the conflict was still in progress and under the strictest censorship rules. Accordingly they are frequently lacking in completeness.

An understanding of the naval war is almost impossible without reference to Bernard Brodie's *Guide to*

Naval Strategy; the diplomatic and strategic background is well covered in Captain E. M. Zacharias' *Secret Missions.* At the close of the conflict Japanese naval officers were carefully interrogated and the U. S. Navy Department published the results of these interrogations in three volumes entitled *Interrogations of Japanese Officials,* Volumes I and II, and *The Campaigns of the Pacific War.* A general running account of naval events is furnished by Gilbert Cant's two books, *America's Navy in World War II* and *The Great Pacific Victory.*

Special accounts of naval events will be found in R. J. Casey's *Torpedo Junction;* C. E. Dickinson's *The Flying Guns* (both for the carrier actions up to Midway); J. Bryan's *Mission Beyond Darkness* (Battle of the Philippine Sea); R. W. Sherrod's *Tarawa;* Stanley Johnston's *Queen of the Flat Tops* (Coral Sea); R. J. Casey's *Battle Below* (submarines); C. Vann Woodward's *Battle for Leyte Gulf;* and J. A. Fields' *The Japanese at Leyte Gulf.*

All of the U. S. Marine Divisions, nearly all of the Army Divisions and many individual ships of the U. S. Navy have produced unit histories. They are of varying merit but should not be neglected by anyone wishing to go into the subject thoroughly. A good running general conspectus appeared during the war in *Foreign Policy Reports,* the work of Hanson W. Baldwin.

INDEX